Miami Marlins 2020

A Baseball Companion

Edited by R.J. Anderson, Craig Goldstein and Bret Sayre

Baseball Prospectus

Craig Brown, Steven Goldman and David Pease, Consultant Editors
Robert Au, Harry Pavlidis and Amy Pircher, Statistics Editors

Copyright © 2020 by DIY Baseball, LLC.
All rights reserved

This book or any part thereof may not be reproduced or transmitted in any form or by any means, electronic or mechanical, including photocopying, recording, or by any information storage and retrieval system, without permission in writing from the publisher.

Limit of Liability/Disclaimer of Warranty: While the publisher and the author have used their best efforts in preparing this book, they make no representations or warranties with respect to the accuracy or completeness of the contents of this book and specifically disclaim any implied warranties of merchantability or fitness for a particular purpose. No warranty may be created or extended by sales representatives or written sales materials. The advice and strategies contained herein may not be suitable for your situation. You should consult with a professional where appropriate. Neither the publisher nor the author shall be liable for any loss of profit or any other commercial damages, including but not limited to special, incidental, consequential, or other damages.

Library of Congress Cataloging-in-Publication Data:
paperback
ISBN-13: 978-1-950716-06-7

Project Credits
Cover Design: Michael Byzewski at Aesthetic Apparatus
Interior Design and Production: Jeff Pease, Dave Pease
Layout: Jeff Pease, Dave Pease

Baseball icon courtesy of Uberux, from https://www.shareicon.net/author/uberux

Ballpark diagram courtesy of Lou Spirito/THIRTY81 Project, https://thirty81project.com/

Manufactured in the United States of America
10 9 8 7 6 5 4 3 2 1

Table of Contents

Statistical Introduction v

Part 1: Team Analysis

Miami Marlins: Where Are You Going, Where Have You Been? 3
 Matthew Trueblood and Keanan Lamb

Performance Graphs 7

2019 Team Performance 8

2020 Team Projections 9

Team Personnel 10

Marlins Park Stats 11

Marlins Team Analysis 13

Part 2: Player Analysis

Marlins Player Analysis 20

Marlins Prospects 95

Part 3: Featured Articles

The Baseball Is Juiced (Again) 111
 Robert Arthur

The Moral Hazard of Playing It Safe 115
 Craig Goldstein

Index of Names 121

Statistical Introduction

Sports are, fundamentally, a blend of athletic endeavor and storytelling. Baseball, like any other sport, tells its stories in so many ways: in the arc of a game from the stands or a season from the box scores, in photos, or even in numbers. At Baseball Prospectus, we understand that statistics don't replace observation or any of baseball's stories, but complement everything else that makes the game so much fun.

What stats help us with is with patterns and precision, variance and value. This book can help you learn things you may not see from watching a game or hundred, whether it's the path of a career over time or the breadth of the entire MLB. We'd also never ask you to choose between our numbers and the experience of viewing a game from the cheap seats or the comfort of your home; our publication combines running the numbers with observations and wisdom from some of the brightest minds we can find. But if you *do* want to learn more about the numbers beyond what's on the backs of player jerseys, let us help explain.

Offense

We've revised our methodology for determining batting value. Long-time readers of the book will notice that we've retired True Average in favor of a new metric: Deserved Runs Created Plus (DRC+). Developed by Jonathan Judge and our stats team, this statistic measures everything a player does at the plate–reaching base, hitting for power, making outs, and moving runners over–and puts it on a scale where 100 equals league-average performance. A DRC+ of 150 is terrific, a DRC+ of 100 is average and a DRC+ of 75 means you better be an excellent defender.

DRC+ also does a better job than any of our previous metrics in taking contextual factors into account. The model adjusts for how the park affects performance, but also for things like the talent of the opposing pitcher, value of different types of batted-ball events, league, temperature and other factors. It's able to describe a player's expected offensive contribution than any other statistic we've found over the years, and also does a better job of predicting future performance as well.

There's a lot more to DRC+'s story, and you can read all about it in greater depth near the end of this book.

The other aspect of run-scoring is baserunning, which we quantify using Baserunning Runs. BRR not only records the value of stolen bases (or getting caught in the act), but also accounts for all the stuff that doesn't show up on the back of a baseball card: a runner's ability to go first to third on a single, or advance on a fly ball.

Defense

Where offensive value is *relatively* easy to identify and understand, defensive value is...not. Over the past dozen years, the sabermetric community has focused mostly on stats based on zone data: a real-live human person records the type of batted ball and estimated landing location, and models are created that give expected outs. From there, you can compare fielders' actual outs to those expected ones. Simple, right?

Unfortunately, zone data has two major issues. First, zone data is recorded by commercial data providers who keep the raw data private unless you pay for it. (All the statistics we build in this book and on our website use public data as inputs.) That hurts our ability to test assumptions or duplicate results. Second, over the years it has become apparent that there's quite a bit of "noise" in zone-based fielding analysis. Sometimes the conclusions drawn from zone data don't hold up to scrutiny, and sometimes the different data provided by different providers don't look anything alike, giving wildly different results. Sometimes the hard-working professional stringers or scorers might unknowingly inflict unconscious bias into the mix: for example good fielders will often be credited with more expected outs despite the data, and ballparks with high press boxes tend to score more line drives than ones with a lower press box.

Enter our Fielding Runs Above Average (FRAA). For most positions, FRAA is built from play-by-play data, which allows us to avoid the subjectivity found in many other fielding metrics. The idea is this: count how many fielding plays are made by a given player and compare that to expected plays for an average fielder at their position (based on pitcher ground ball tendencies and batter handedness). Then we adjust for park and base-out situations.

When it comes to catchers, our methodology is a little different thanks to the laundry list of responsibilities they're tasked with beyond just, well, catching and throwing the ball. By now you've probably heard about "framing" or the art of making umpires more likely to call balls outside the strike zone for strikes. To put this into one tidy number, we incorporate pitch tracking data (for the years it exists) and adjust for important factors like pitcher, umpire, batter and home-field advantage using a mixed-model approach. This grants us a number for how many strikes the catcher is personally adding to (or subtracting from) his pitchers' performance...which we then convert to runs added or lost using linear weights.

Framing is one of the biggest parts of determining catcher value, but we also take into account blocking balls from going past, whether a scorer deems it a passed ball or a wild pitch. We use a similar approach—one that really benefits from the pitch tracking data that tells us what ends up in the dirt and what doesn't. We also include a catcher's ability to prevent stolen bases and how well they field balls in play, and *finally* we come up with our FRAA for catchers.

Pitching

Both pitching and fielding make up the half of baseball that isn't run scoring: run prevention. Separating pitching from fielding is a tough task, and most recent pitching analysis has branched off from Voros McCracken's famous (and controversial) statement, "There is little if any difference among major-league pitchers in their ability to prevent hits on balls hit in the field of play." The research of the analytic community has validated this to some extent, and there are a host of "defense-independent" pitching measures that have been developed to try and extract the effect of the defense behind a hurler from the pitcher's work.

Our solution to this quandary is Deserved Run Average (DRA), our core pitching metric. DRA looks like earned run average (ERA), the tried-and-true pitching stat you've seen on every baseball broadcast or box score from the past century, but it's very different. To start, DRA takes an event-by-event look at what the pitchers does, and adjusts the value of that event based on different environmental factors like park, batter, catcher, umpire, base-out situation, run differential, inning, defense, home field advantage, pitcher role and temperature. That mixed model gives us a pitcher's expected contribution, similar to what we do for our DRC+ model for hitters and FRAA model for catchers. (Oh, and we also consider the pitcher's effect on basestealing and on balls getting past the catcher.)

It's important to note that DRA is set to the scale of runs allowed per nine innings (RA9) instead of ERA, which makes DRA's scale slightly higher than ERA's. The reason for this is because ERA tends to overrate three types of pitchers:

1. Pitchers who play in parks where scorers hand out more errors. Official scorers differ significantly in the frequency at which they assign errors to fielders.
2. Ground-ball pitchers, because a substantial proportion of errors occur on groundballs.
3. Pitchers who aren't very good. Better pitchers often allow fewer unearned runs than bad pitchers, because good pitchers tend to find ways to get out of jams.

Since the last time you picked up an edition of this book, we've also made a few minor changes to DRA to make it better. Recent research into "tunneling"—the act of throwing consecutive pitches that appear similar from a batter's point of view until after the swing decision point–data has given us a new contextual factor to account for in DRA: plate distance. This refers to the distance between successive pitches as they approach the plate, and while it has a smaller effect than factors like velocity or whiff rate, it still can help explain pitcher strikeout rate in our model.

New Pitching Metrics for 2020

We're including a few "new" pitching metrics in the book for the 2020 edition, though unlike last year, these numbers may be a little bit more familiar to those of you who have spent some time investigating baseball statistics.

Fastball Percentage

Our fastball percentage (FB%) statistic measures how frequently a pitcher throws a pitch classified as a "fastball," measured as a percentage of overall pitches thrown. We qualify three types of fastballs:

1. The traditional four-seam fastball;
2. The two-seam fastball or sinker;
3. "Hard cutters," which are pitches that have the movement profile of a cut fastball and are used as the pitcher's primary offering or in place of a more traditional fastball.

For example, a pitcher with a FB% of 67 throws any combination of these three pitches about two-thirds of the time.

Whiff Rate

Everybody loves a swing and a miss, and whiff rate (WHF) measures how frequently pitchers induce a swinging strike. To calculate WHF, we add up all the pitches thrown that ended with a swinging strike, then divide that number by a pitcher's total pitches thrown. Most often, high whiff rates correlate with high strikeout rates (and overall effective pitcher performance).

Called Strike Probability

Called Strike Probability (CSP) is a number that represents the likelihood that all of a pitcher's pitches will be called a strike while controlling for location, pitcher and batter handedness, umpire and count. Here's how it works: on each pitch, our model determines how many times (out of 100) that a similar pitch was called for a strike given those factors mentioned above, and when normalized for each batter's strike zone. Then we average the CSP for all pitches thrown by a pitcher in a season, and that gives us the yearly CSP percentage you see in the stats boxes.

As you might imagine, pitchers with a higher CSP are more likely to work in the zone, where pitchers with a lower CSP are likely locating their pitches outside the normal strike zone, for better or for worse.

Projections

Many of you aren't turning to this book just for a look at what a player has done, but for a look at what a player is going to do: the PECOTA projections. PECOTA, initially developed by Nate Silver (who has moved on to greater fame as a political analyst), consists of three parts:

1. Major-league equivalencies, which use minor-league statistics to project how a player will perform in the major leagues;
2. Baseline forecasts, which use weighted averages and regression to the mean to estimate a player's current true talent level; and
3. Aging curves, which uses the career paths of comparable players to estimate how a player's statistics are likely to change over time.

With all those important things covered, let's take a look at what's in the book this year.

Team Prospectus

Most of this book is composed of team chapters, with one for each of the 30 major-league franchises. On the first page of each chapter, you'll see a box that contains some of the key statistics for each team as well as a very inviting stadium diagram. (You can see an example of this for the Milwaukee Brewers on this very page!)

We start with the team name, their unadjusted 2019 win-loss record, and their divisional ranking. Beneath that are a host of other team statistics. **Pythag** presents an adjusted 2019 winning percentage, calculated by taking runs scored per game (**RS/G**) and runs allowed per game (**RA/G**) for the team, and running them through a version of Bill James' Pythagorean formula that was refined and improved by David Smyth and Brandon Heipp. (The formula is called "Pythagenpat," which is equally fun to type and to say.)

Next up is **DRC+**, described earlier, to indicate the overall hitting ability of the team either above or below league-average. Run prevention on the pitching side is covered by **DRA** (also mentioned earlier) and another metric: Fielding Independent Pitching (**FIP**), which calculates another ERA-like statistic based on strikeouts, walks, and home runs recorded. Defensive Efficiency Rating (**DER**) tells us the percentage of balls in play turned into outs for the team, and is a quick fielding shorthand that rounds out run prevention.

After that, we have several measures related to roster composition, as opposed to on-field performance. **B-Age** and **P-Age** tell us the average age of a team's batters and pitchers, respectively. **Salary** is the combined team payroll for all on-field players, and Doug Pappas' Marginal Dollars per Marginal Win (**M$/MW**) tells us how much money a team spent to earn production above replacement level.

Ending this batch of statistics is the number of disabled list days a team had over the season (**IL Days**) and the amount of salary paid to players on the disabled list (**$ on IL**); this final number is expressed as a percentage of total payroll.

Next to each of these stats, we've listed each team's MLB rank in that category from first to 30th. In this, first always indicates a positive outcome and 30th a negative outcome, except in the case of salary—first is highest.

After the franchise statistics, we share a few items about the team's home ballpark. There's the aforementioned diagram of the park's dimensions (including distances to the outfield wall), a graphic showing the height of the wall from the left-field pole to the right-field pole, and a table showing three-year park factors for the stadium. The park factors are displayed as indexes where 100 is average, 110 means that the park inflates the statistic in question by 10 percent, and 90 means that the park deflates the statistic in question by 10 percent.

On the second page of each team chapter, you'll find three graphs. The first is the **2019 Hit List Ranking**. This shows our Hit List Rank for the team on each day of the 2019 season and is intended to give you a picture of the ups and downs of the team's season. Hit List Rank measures overall team performance and drives the Hit List Power Rankings at the baseballprospectus.com website.

The second graph is **Committed Payroll** and helps you see how the team's payroll has compared to the MLB and divisional average payrolls over time. Payroll figures are current as of January 1, 2020; with so many free agents still unsigned as of this writing, the final 2020 figure will likely be significantly different for many teams. (In the meantime, you can always find the most current data at Baseball Prospectus' Cot's Baseball Contracts page.)

The third graph is **Farm System Ranking** and displays how the Baseball Prospectus prospect team has ranked the organization's farm system since 2007.

After the graphs, we have a **Personnel** section that lists many of the important decision-makers and upper-level field and operations staff members for the franchise, as well as any former Baseball Prospectus staff members who are currently part of the organization. (In very rare circumstances, someone might be on both lists!)

Juan Soto LF

Born: 10/25/98   Age: 21   Bats: L   Throws: L
Height: 6'1"   Weight: 185   Origin: International Free Agent, 2015

YEAR	TEAM	LVL	AGE	PA	R	2B	3B	HR	RBI	BB	K	SB	CS	AVG/OBP/SLG
2017	NAT	RK	18	27	3	1	1	0	4	2	1	0	0	.320/.370/.440
2017	HAG	A	18	96	15	5	0	3	14	10	8	1	2	.360/.427/.523
2018	HAG	A	19	74	12	5	3	5	24	14	13	2	0	.373/.486/.814
2018	POT	A+	19	73	17	3	1	7	18	11	8	0	1	.371/.466/.790
2018	HAR	AA	19	35	4	2	0	2	10	4	7	1	0	.323/.400/.581
2018	WAS	MLB	19	494	77	25	1	22	70	79	99	5	2	.292/.406/.517
2019	WAS	MLB	20	659	110	32	5	34	110	108	132	12	1	.282/.401/.548
2020	WAS	MLB	21	630	92	30	3	35	102	85	123	5	2	.284/.382/.543

Comparables: Ronald Acuña Jr., Mike Trout, Tony Conigliaro

YEAR	TEAM	LVL	AGE	PA	DRC+	VORP	BABIP	BRR	FRAA	WARP
2017	NAT	RK	18	27	135	1.5	.333	0.0	RF(9): -1.1	0.0
2017	HAG	A	18	96	181	8.0	.373	1.0	RF(19): -1.9, LF(2): -0.3	0.9
2018	HAG	A	19	74	222	14.5	.405	0.3	RF(14): 1.1, CF(2): 0.2	1.2
2018	POT	A+	19	73	260	15.4	.340	1.4	RF(14): 1.0, LF(1): 0.0	1.6
2018	HAR	AA	19	35	113	3.6	.364	0.0	LF(4): 0.6, RF(4): -0.5	0.1
2018	WAS	MLB	19	494	125	40.5	.338	-0.5	LF(114): 2.7	3.0
2019	WAS	MLB	20	659	136	49.0	.312	1.4	LF(150): -0.8	4.9
2020	WAS	MLB	21	630	133	43.6	.310	-0.1	LF 3	4.8

Position Players

After all that information and a thoughtful bylined essay covering each team, we present our player comments. These are also bylined, but due to frequent franchise shifts during the offseason, our bylines are more a rough guide than a perfect accounting of who wrote what.

Each player is listed with the major-league team that employed him as of early January 2020. If a player changed teams after that point via free agency, trade, or any other method, you'll be able to find them in the chapter for their previous squad.

As an example, take a look at the player comment for Nationals outfielder Juan Soto: the stat block that accompanies his written comment is at the top of this page. First we cover biographical information (age is as of June 30, 2020) before moving onto the stats themselves. Our statistic columns include standard identifying information like **YEAR**, **TEAM**, **LVL** (level of affiliated play) and **AGE** before getting into the numbers. Next, we provide raw, untranslated numbers like you might find on the back of your dad's baseball cards: **PA** (plate appearances), **R** (runs), **2B** (doubles), **3B** (triples), **HR** (home runs), **RBI** (runs batted in), **BB** (walks), **K** (strikeouts), **SB** (stolen bases) and **CS** (caught stealing).

Next, we have unadjusted "slash" statistics: **AVG** (batting average), **OBP** (on-base percentage) and **SLG** (slugging percentage). Following the slash line is **DRC+** (Deserved Runs Created Plus), which we described earlier as total offensive expected contribution compared to the league average.

One of our oldest active metrics, **VORP** (Value Over Replacement Player), considers offensive production, position and plate appearances. In essence, it is the number of runs contributed beyond what a replacement-level player at the same position would contribute if given the same percentage of team plate appearances. VORP does not consider the quality of a player's defense.

BABIP (batting average on balls in play) tells us how often a ball in play fell for a hit, and can help us identify whether a batter may have been lucky or not...but note that high BABIPs also tend to follow the great hitters of our time, as well as speedy singles hitters who put the ball on the ground.

The next item is **BRR** (Baserunning Runs), which covers all of a player's baserunning accomplishments including (but not limited to) swiped bags and failed attempts. Next is **FRAA** (Fielding Runs Above Average), which also includes the number of games previously played at each position noted in parentheses. Multi-position players have only their two most frequent positions listed here, but their total FRAA number reflects all positions played.

Our last column here is **WARP** (Wins Above Replacement Player). WARP estimates the total value of a player, which means for hitters it takes into account hitting runs above average (calculated using the DRC+ model), BRR and FRAA. Then, it makes an adjustment for positions played and gives the player a credit for plate appearances based upon the difference between "replacement level"—which is derived from the quality of players added to a team's roster after the start of the season–and the league average.

The final line just below the stats box is **PECOTA** data, which is discussed further in a following section.

Catchers

Catchers are a special breed, and thus they have earned their own separate box which displays some of the defensive metrics that we've built just for them. As an example, let's check out J.T. Realmuto.

The **YEAR** and **TEAM** columns match what you'd find in the other stat box. **P. COUNT** indicates the number of pitches thrown while the catcher was behind the plate, including swinging strikes, fouls and balls in play. **FRM RUNS** is the total run value the catcher provided (or cost) his team by influencing the umpire to call strikes where other catchers did not. **BLK RUNS** expresses the total run value above or below average for the catcher's ability to prevent wild pitches and passed balls. **THRW RUNS** is calculated using a similar model as the previous two statistics, and it measures a catcher's ability to throw out basestealers but also to dissuade them from testing his arm in the first place. It takes into account factors like the pitcher (including his delivery and pickoff move) and baserunner (who could be as fast as Billy Hamilton or as slow as Yonder Alonso). **TOT RUNS** is the sum of all of the previous three statistics.

Justin Verlander   RHP

Born: 02/20/83   Age: 37   Bats: R   Throws: R
Height: 6'5"   Weight: 225   Origin: Round 1, 2004 Draft (#2 overall)

YEAR	TEAM	LVL	AGE	W	L	SV	G	GS	IP	H	HR	BB/9	K/9	K	GB%	BABIP
2017	DET	MLB	34	10	8	0	28	28	172	153	23	3.5	9.2	176	34%	.283
2017	HOU	MLB	34	5	0	0	5	5	34	17	4	1.3	11.4	43	32%	.194
2018	HOU	MLB	35	16	9	0	34	34	214	156	28	1.6	12.2	290	31%	.272
2019	HOU	MLB	36	21	6	0	34	34	223	137	36	1.7	12.1	300	36%	.219
2020	HOU	MLB	37	15	6	0	29	29	184	138	28	2.3	12.1	248	35%	.274

Comparables: Zack Greinke, A.J. Burnett, Aníbal Sánchez

YEAR	TEAM	LVL	AGE	WHIP	ERA	DRA	WARP	MPH	FB%	WHF	CSP
2017	DET	MLB	34	1.28	3.82	4.03	3.0	97.7	58	11	47.8
2017	HOU	MLB	34	0.65	1.06	3.08	0.9	97.5	59.6	15.1	49.9
2018	HOU	MLB	35	0.90	2.52	2.33	7.3	97.5	61.2	16.2	51.6
2019	HOU	MLB	36	0.80	2.58	2.51	7.9	96.8	49.9	17.5	48.3
2020	HOU	MLB	37	1.01	2.75	2.95	5.3	95.8	54.6	15.1	48.2

Pitchers

Let's give our pitchers a turn, using 2019 AL Cy Young winner Justin Verlander as our example. Take a look at his stat block: the first line and the **YEAR**, **TEAM**, **LVL** and **AGE** columns are the same as in the position player example earlier.

Here too, we have a series of columns that display raw, unadjusted statistics compiled by the pitcher over the course of a season: **W** (wins), **L** (losses), **SV** (saves), **G** (games pitched), **GS** (games started), **IP** (innings pitched), **H** (hits allowed) and **HR** (home runs allowed). Next we have two statistics that are rates: **BB/9** (walks per nine innings) and **K/9** (strikeouts per nine innings), before returning to the unadjusted K (strikeouts).

Next up is **GB%** (ground ball percentage), which is the percentage of all batted balls that were hit on the ground, including both outs and hits. Remember, this is based on observational data and subject to human error, so please approach this with a healthy dose of skepticism.

BABIP (batting average on balls in play) is calculated using the same methodology as it is for position players, but it often tells us more about a pitcher than it does a hitter. With pitchers, a high BABIP is often due to poor defense or bad luck, and can often be an indicator of potential rebound, and a low BABIP may be cause to expect performance regression. (A typical league-average BABIP is close to .290-.300.)

The metrics **WHIP** (walks plus hits per inning pitched) and **ERA** (earned run average) are old standbys: WHIP measures walks and hits allowed on a per-inning basis, while ERA measures earned runs on a nine-inning basis. Neither of these stats are translated or adjusted.

DRA (Deserved Run Average) was described at length earlier, and measures how many runs the pitcher "deserved" to allow per nine innings. Please note that since we lack all the data points that would make for a "real" DRA for minor-league events, the DRA displayed for minor league partial-seasons is based off of different data. (That data is a modified version of our cFIP metric, which you can find more information about on our website.)

Just like with hitters, **WARP** (Wins Above Replacement Player) is a total value metric that puts pitchers of all stripes on the same scale as position players. We use DRA as the primary input for our calculation of WARP. You might notice that relief pitchers (due to their limited innings) may have a lower WARP than you were expecting or than you might see in other WARP-like metrics. WARP does not take leverage into account, just the actions a pitcher performs and the expected value of those actions...which ends up judging high-leverage relief pitchers differently than you might imagine given their prestige and market value.

MPH gives you the pitcher's 95th percentile velocity for the noted season, in order to give you an idea of what the *peak* fastball velocity a pitcher possesses. Since this comes from our pitch-tracking data, it is not publicly available for minor-league pitchers.

Finally, we display the three new pitching metrics we described earlier. **FB%** (fastball percentage) gives you the percentage of fastballs thrown out of all pitches. **WHF** (whiff rate) tells you the percentage of swinging strikes induced out of all pitches. **CSP** (called strike probability) expresses the likelihood of all pitches thrown to result in a called strike, after controlling for factors like handedness, umpire, pitch type, count and location.

PECOTA

All players have PECOTA projections for 2020, as well as a set of other numbers that describe the performance of comparable players according to PECOTA. All projections for 2020 are for the player at the date we went to press in early January and are projected into the league and park context as indicated by the team abbreviation. (Note that players at very low levels of the minors are too unpredictable to assess using these numbers.) All PECOTA projected statistics represent a player's projected major-league performance.

Below the projections are the player's three highest-scoring comparable players as determined by PECOTA. All comparables represent a snapshot of how the listed player was performing at the same age as the current player, so if a

23-year-old pitcher is compared to Bartolo Colón, he's actually being compared to a 23-year-old Colón, not the version that pitched for the Rangers in 2018, nor to Colón's career as a whole.

A few points about pitcher projections. First, we aren't yet projecting peak velocity, so that column will be blank in the PECOTA lines. Second, projecting DRA is trickier than evaluating past performance, because it is unclear how deserving each pitcher will be of his anticipated outcomes. However, we know that another DRA-related statistic–contextual FIP or cFIP–estimates future run scoring very well. So for PECOTA, the projected DRA figures you see are based on the past cFIPs generated by the pitcher and comparable players over time, along with the other factors described above.

Lineouts

In each chapter's Lineouts section, you'll find abbreviated text comments, as well as all the same information you'd find in our full player comments. The only difference is that we limit the stats boxes in this section to only including the 2019 information for each player.

Managers

After all those wonderful team chapters, we've got statistics for each big-league manager, all of whom are organized by alphabetical order. Here you'll find a block including an extraordinary amount of information collected from each manager's entire career. For more information on the acronyms and what they mean, please visit the Glossary at www.baseballprospectus.com.

There is one important metric that we'd like to call attention to, and you'll find it next to each manager's name: **wRM+** (weighted reliever management plus). Developed by Rob Arthur and Rian Watt, wRM+ investigates how good a manager is at using their best relievers during the moments of highest leverage, using both our proprietary DRA metric as well as Leverage Index. wRM+ is scaled to a league average of 100, and a wRM+ of 105 indicates that relievers were used approximately five percent "better" than average. On the other hand, a wRM+ of 95 would tell us the team used its relievers five percent "worse" than the average team.

While wRM+ does not have an extremely strong correlation with a manager, it is statistically significant; this means that a manager is not *entirely* responsible for a team's wRM+, but does have some effect on that number.

PECOTA Leaderboards

If you're familiar with PECOTA, then you'll have noticed that the projection system often appears bullish on players coming off a bad year and bearish on players coming off a good year. (This is because the system weights several previous seasons, not just the most recent one.) In addition, we publish the 50th

Miami Marlins 2020

percentile projections for each player–which is smack in the middle of the range of projected production—which tends to mean PECOTA stat lines don't often have extreme results like 40 home runs or 250 strikeouts in a given season. In essence, PECOTA doesn't project very many extreme seasons.

At the end of the book, we've ranked the top players at each position based on their PECOTA projections. This might help you visualize just how a given player's projection compares to that of their peers, so that even if a dramatic stat line isn't projected, you can still imagine how they stack up against the rest of the league.

xvi - Statistical Introduction

Part 1: Team Analysis

Miami Marlins: Where Are You Going, Where Have You Been?

Matthew Trueblood and Keanan Lamb

2019: What Went Right

The Marlins did not enter 2019 with any hope of contending for anything. In an exceptionally deep and competitive division, they stood out like a sore thumb. Miami never intended to use the standings to define success or failure this year, and despite their miserable record, there have been a bunch of positive storylines. The club asked their fans to judge the campaign on a crop of young pitchers about whom they were very excited, and those pitchers almost universally lived up to their billing—and then some.

Caleb Smith's real breakout came in 2018, but last season cemented his status as a candidate for the front of the rotation when the Marlins are again knocking on the door of the playoffs. He missed a month in the middle of the year and was greatly diminished after his return (a 6.39 ERA over his final 11 starts), but all told, he continued to demonstrate a feel for three above-average pitches. Sandy Alcantara made the All-Star team, emerged as a respected young leader for a team that needed that kind of presence, and showed some of the best pure stuff in the organization. Pablo López had a season marred by injury, but was even better than Smith when on the mound (a 4.19 DRA versus 4.55 for Smith), cementing the improvements he hinted at in 2018.

Then there were the players who served as throw-ins when the Marlins dealt Marcell Ozuna and Christian Yelich over the winter of 2017-18. Jordan Yamamoto, the third or fourth piece in the Yelich deal, split his season between Double-A Jacksonville and Miami, acquitting himself admirably at both stops. Zac Gallen, a little-known element of the Ozuna deal that also brought over Alcantara, had such an extraordinary run in the laughably hitter-friendly Pacific Coast League that he forced his way to Miami for seven starts—and then brought back slugging shortstop prospect Jazz Chisholm in a surprising deadline deal with the Diamondbacks. If Gallen hadn't broken out so impressively, he'd never have netted them Chisholm, but just as importantly, the Marlins couldn't have traded Gallen in good faith if they hadn't gotten such encouraging work from Smith, López, Alcantara and Yamamoto.

The team got creative to complete the Gallen deal and proved even more nimble in trading away two key relievers. By packaging a mid-tier pitching prospect with veteran reliever Sergio Romo, they were able to get Twins first base prospect Lewin Díaz. Then, they flipped winter addition (and star-caliber relief ace) Nick Anderson, along with superfluous swingman Trevor Richards, to Tampa Bay for power reliever Ryne Stanek and slugging outfield prospect Jesús Sánchez. There's room to argue with the underlying logic on some of those moves, and indeed, the Anderson one feels very risky, but the Marlins executed their broader strategy well, and it was made possible by the way their in-house pitching options blossomed throughout the spring and summer.

On the offensive side, Brian Anderson was more or less who they expect him to be, and Miguel Rojas underwent a quieter version of Nick Ahmed's 2019 transformation, from an elite defensive shortstop who can't hit to a more well-rounded offensive player whose offense no longer swallows the value of his defense.

2019: What Went Wrong

Anderson and Rojas are the only things resembling, in any remote way, bright spots at the plate. The players who were supposed to prop up the offense, to make it a representative major league-caliber unit and/or provide hope for the future, were an unmitigated catastrophe. Veterans Starlin Castro, Curtis Granderson, Martin Prado and Neil Walker combined for a total of 1.0 WARP despite nearly 1,400 plate appearances. The two batters the team hoped would announce themselves as long-term pieces of the positional core, Jorge Alfaro and Lewis Brinson, instead announced themselves as stopgaps who will need to be replaced before the team can move forward. Brinson has played his way out of any serious consideration as a future regular, anywhere in MLB. Alfaro disappointed at the plate and battled significant injuries, including a concussion.

The Fish had a few late-blooming, bat-first players about whom they were modestly excited in Garrett Cooper, Peter O'Brien, and Jon Berti. They gambled on the tools of busted ex-prospects Harold Ramírez and Rosell Herrera. They fired their hitting coach. They called up Isan Díaz for (they hoped) a jolt of power and prospect panache in August. None of it worked. None of it came close to working. None of it threatened to work in the way that almost every bad team has a few bad ideas that threaten to work. There is no credible evidence that the Marlins are within even four or five good hitters of being a good offensive team. Their 79 team DRC+ was the worst in the majors and places them as about as productive, relative to their competition, as were the 1936 Mets or the 1933 St. Louis Browns. It was that bad. —*Matthew Trueblood*

Prospect Outlook

A rebuild of the farm system does not happen overnight, although the is quickly coming together as one of the more prospect-laden orgs in the game. Remember: not so long ago they were quick to jettison future studs like Chris Paddack, Luis Castillo, and Josh Naylor for veteran also-rans that left the farm barren.

Mixing in high draft picks with trade acquisitions, there is both top-end pedigree and depth featured up and down the system. In 2020, it is conceivable that 10 of their top 20 prospects make their debuts, led by right-handed starter **Sixto Sánchez**. While still building up a season-long starter's workload, another strong campaign would have him knocking on the door, as well as fellow acquisitions outfielder **Jesús Sánchez** and shortstop **Jazz Chisholm**.

With so much young talent towards the upper levels, and a fair amount at High-A and below, there is no rush for management to push anyone. One name to know beyond the top ten is first basemen **Lewin Díaz**, who had a breakout 2019 season and could contend to be the team's starter next season. —*Keanan Lamb*

2020 Outlook

To their credit, the Marlins didn't ignore their pressing need for a positional overhaul. They still went about solving it the way a rebuilding team that understands itself to be far from contention would, but let no one say they sat idle. Jonathan Villar, Corey Dickerson, Jesús Aguilar, Francisco Cervelli, and Matt Joyce all will get chances to play often and shore up a lineup that had too many holes and too little variety.

It's no surprise that the team left that rotation alone. It's important not only that they continue to see what each of their current crop of young arms can do, but that they leave room for the fairly imminent arrival of even more help on the mound. However, their bullpen was a shambles, and adding Brandon Kintzler (plus Yimi García, Rule 5 selection Sterling Sharp, and Stephen Tarpley) to the mix mitigates some of the risk associated with such a glaring weakness. All eyes are still fixed on some year beyond 2020 in Miami, but these moves could yield something in trade in a few months, and they'll make the team somewhat less embarrassing in the meantime. —*Matthew Trueblood*

Performance Graphs

2019 Hit List Ranking

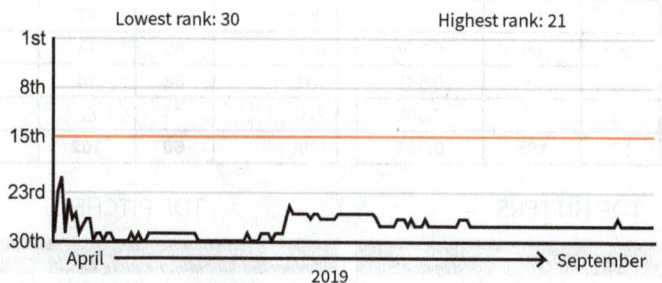

Committed Payroll (in millions)

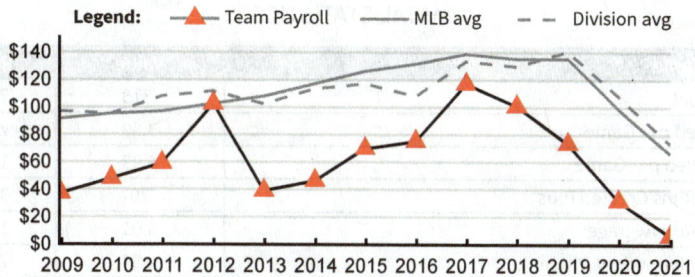

Farm System Ranking

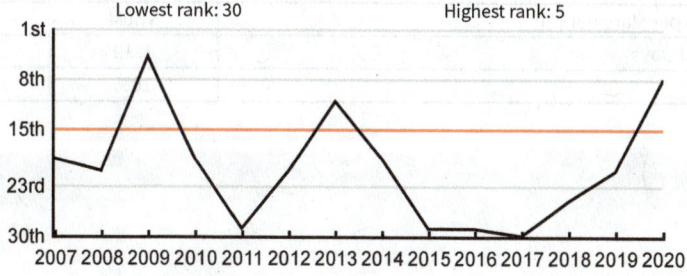

2019 Team Performance

ACTUAL STANDINGS

Team	W	L	Pct
ATL	97	65	0.599
WAS	93	69	0.574
NYN	86	76	0.531
PHI	81	81	0.500
MIA	**57**	**105**	**0.352**

THIRD-ORDER STANDINGS

Team	W	L	Pct
WAS	95	67	0.584
ATL	89	73	0.550
NYN	88	74	0.542
PHI	74	88	0.457
MIA	**60**	**102**	**0.373**

TOP HITTERS

Player	WARP
Brian Anderson	3.1
Miguel Rojas	1.4
Garrett Cooper	1.2

TOP PITCHERS

Player	WARP
Sandy Alcantara	2.6
Caleb Smith	2.0
Pablo López	1.9

VITAL STATISTICS

Statistic Name	Value	Rank
Pythagenpat	.375	28th
Runs Scored per Game	3.80	29th
Runs Allowed per Game	4.99	19th
Deserved Runs Created Plus	79	30th
Deserved Run Average	5.01	19th
Fielding Independent Pitching	4.84	21st
Defensive Efficiency Rating	.719	4th
Batter Age	28.4	22nd
Pitcher Age	26.2	2nd
Salary	$71.9M	29th
Marginal $ per Marginal Win	$7.0M	4th
Injured List Days	1219	20th
$ on IL	10%	4th

2020 Team Projections

PROJECTED STANDINGS

Team	W	L	Pct	+/-
NYN	87.8	74.2	0.542	2
WAS	87.1	74.9	0.538	-6
ATL	82.8	79.2	0.511	-14
PHI	76.8	85.2	0.474	-4
MIA	**71.3**	**90.7**	**0.440**	**14**

TOP PROJECTED HITTERS

Player	WARP
Brian Anderson	1.8
Corey Dickerson	1.4
Jesús Aguilar	1.2

TOP PROJECTED PITCHERS

Player	WARP
Caleb Smith	2.3
Pablo López	1.8
Sandy Alcantara	1.4

FARM SYSTEM REPORT

Top Prospect	Number of Top 101 Prospects
Sixto Sanchez, #27	5

KEY DEDUCTIONS

Player	WARP
Starlin Castro	0.6
Austin Dean	0.3
Tyler Heineman	0.1
José Quijada	0.1
Neil Walker	0.0
Tyler Kinley	0.0
Kyle Keller	0.0
Jarlin García	0.0
JT Riddle	-0.1
Tayron Guerrero	-0.2

KEY ADDITIONS

Player	WARP
Corey Dickerson	1.4
Jesús Aguilar	1.2
Jonathan Villar	1.1
Lewin Diaz	0.8
Yimi García	0.8
Matt Joyce	0.6
Francisco Cervelli	0.6
Sixto Sanchez	0.6
Brad Boxberger	0.1
Humberto Mejia	0.1

Team Personnel

Chief Executive Officer
Derek Jeter

President of Baseball Operations
Michael Hill

Assistant General Manager
Brian Chattin

Vice President, Player Development and Scouting
Gary Denbo

Manager
Don Mattingly

BP Alumni
John Eshleman

Marlins Park Stats

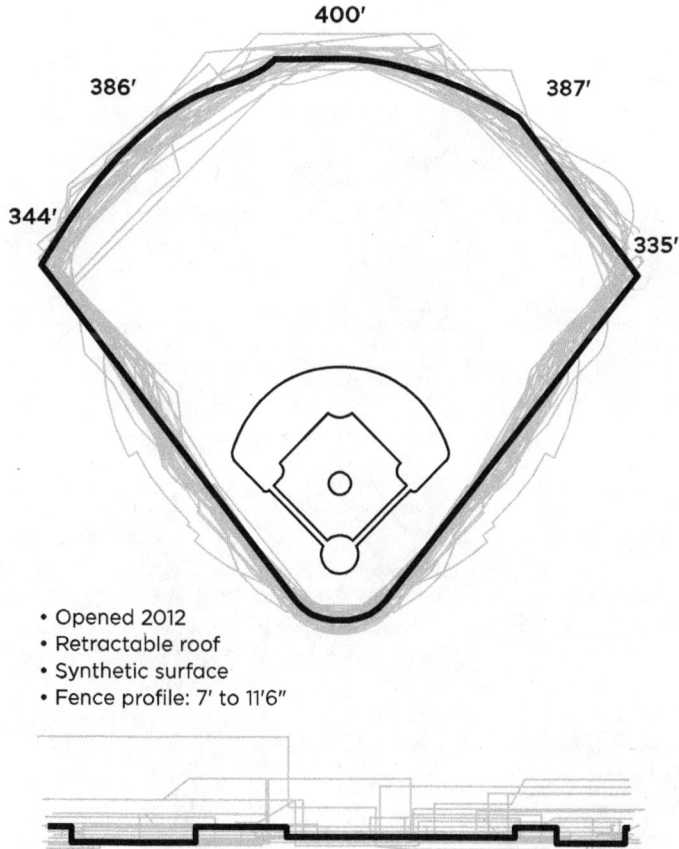

- Opened 2012
- Retractable roof
- Synthetic surface
- Fence profile: 7' to 11'6"

Three-Year Park Factors

Runs	Runs/RH	Runs/LH	HR/RH	HR/LH
95	95	94	87	91

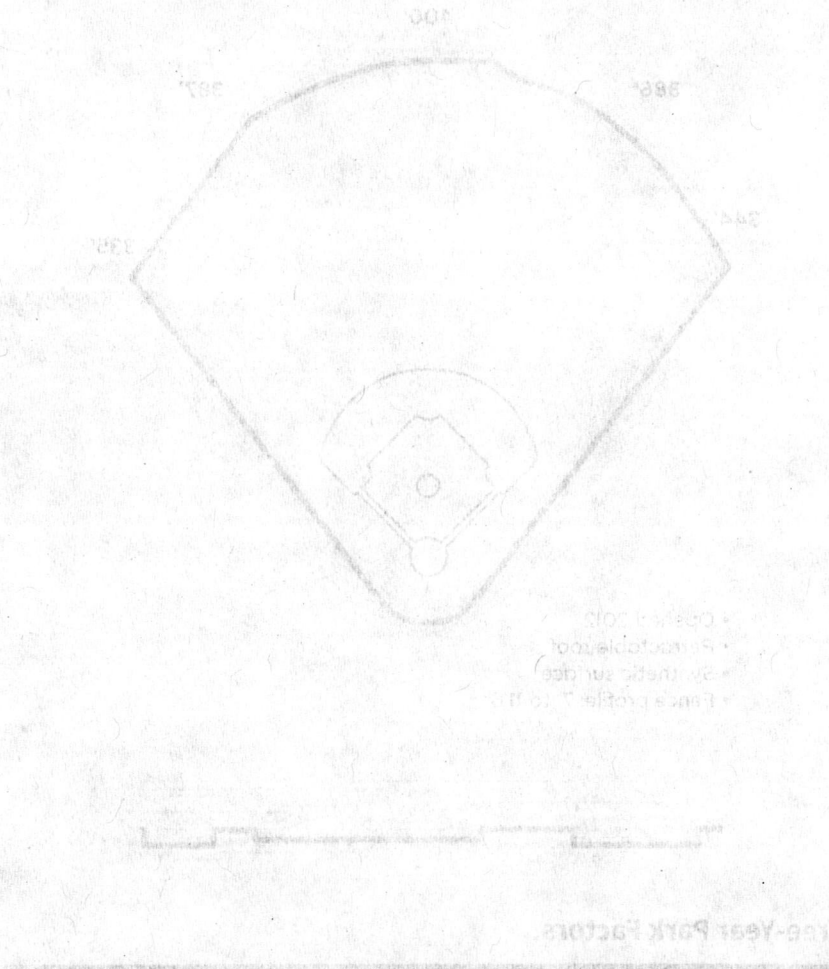

Marlins Team Analysis

If you're the type of person who is about to settle in and read 2,500 words on the 2020 Miami Marlins, I'm going to assume you are also the type of person who has at least once thought about faking your death. So I see immediately what this team's appeal is to you.

> Things haven't been good for a long time. You've become distant and strange. Might as well cut ties with the familiar. Tear it all down. Start over. Inform everyone you haven't been feeling so hot. Announce a sudden interest in an uncharacteristically life-threatening hobby. Disappear in some kind of mountain-unicycling accident. Make yourself unrecognizable. Resurface as another, better you. Begin a new life with a fresh identity. Forget everything that's happened to this point. This is how it's always been.

What you need to fake your death is a plan. An old man in Florida once tried to stage his own murder by tying a gun to a weather balloon. He succeeded in dying, but not in fooling investigators, who, according to the *Tampa Bay Times*, discovered a list of internet searches on his phone like "How to commit Suicide" and "Undetectable suicide methods" and "How many cubic feet of helium do you need to raise one pound?" So you need a better plan than that.

And it seems like the Marlins have one. As of now, their rebuild has moved beyond "no body was recovered among the wreckage" and has reached a phase closer to "shaving in a gas station bathroom and nodding in approval at the altered reflection staring back at them."

More baseball fans than ever are familiar with the "rebuild" process and have become sickened by the term, knowing exactly what it includes, but having long-ago surrendered to its inevitable protocol. And like faking your death, rebuilds are complex and contain multitudes of X-factors. Maybe the people you were basing your plan around aren't as valuable as you thought or some flawed analysis gets your money invested in the wrong thing. Or maybe some long lost neighbor recognizes you on the street and, when they shout your old name, you instinctively turn and look and there's a horrific moment of recognition in which you *both* know that it's you, and you have to decide, there and now, if your plan can survive with a witness out there saying they spotted you in Puerto Christo without your beard.

Miami Marlins 2020

The point is, rebuilding and faking your death are both some of the toughest challenges we'll face in life, but *unlike* faking your death, when you're rebuilding a baseball team, everybody's watching.

Well, not really. Not in South Florida. You will be unsurprised to learn that the Marlins attracted more people than absolutely no one in 2019, with the lowest average attendance by far (just over 10,000). They were the only team in the major leagues to have a total attendance number lower than 1 million for the season, and it wasn't even close (811,302). They will once again have some work to do in getting fans into the stadium, sitting them down, and pointing their heads toward Marlins baseball and saying, "This is a sport some people like. Do you like it? No, you can't leave. This won't end for three and a half hours." Marlins CEO and part-owner Derek Jeter even moved the home run sculpture outside. God forbid the Marlins be known for something other than not having fans.

Just to provide you some context for cost of the Marlins' current roster ($27 million) it's about the price of a mansion in San Francisco, or a large-scale money laundering conspiracy, or the amount that was awarded to a man released from prison after serving 27 years for a murder he didn't commit. The 2020 season will be all about the Yankees, who made a big free agent signing and will be the top story of the league, at least until Rob Manfred announces that MLB is abandoning its attempts to market itself to children and will simply ride out its popularity with upper middle-aged sourpusses until they've all died out. Regardless of what people are talking about in baseball, no one really talks about a team constructed so inexpensively that it costs, in total, about 1/12th of what the Yankees paid Gerrit Cole.

If you're a follower of this team, and if you're reading this I assume you must be—either that or you read all of the other essays already and you're some kind of deranged completist—then you might be sick of sentiments like, "The Marlins? They're bad," or "The Marlins? No thanks," or "The Marlins? They make me want to fake my own death!"

You're likely sick of these sentiments because they're the only things most people have had to say about Miami for years. Every division has its filthy basement, and other than occasional check-ins on how poorly everything is going, the teams inhabiting that basement spend most of the season totally ignored. Miami knew where it was headed when it traded away all of its realest talent a couple of years ago, and everyone watching knew it, too: They held a town hall, and Jeter had to sit there while a line of people took turns insulting him into a microphone. It was the greatest moment in sports history.

Reporters found Jeter again in late August of 2019 at a team event in an elementary school. Jeter said he was frustrated, being a real competitor and all, that the Marlins were still only in this early phase of the rebuild, in which they would lose a ton of games and not have a lot of good players. Later in the off-season, Jeter handed out meals to the community for Thanksgiving in a continuance of his rebrand from "overwhelmed rich person who thought this would be easier" to "benevolent millionaire about town." One can only assume this was *his* attempt at faking his own death and starting over, only without the staged helicopter crash, because let's face it, setting all *that* up probably wound up seeming like *way* too much work, so he settled for some media spin.

When the press talked to him around Thanksgiving, Jeter made it clear through brazen pronouncements and the cutting off of questions that if the Marlins saw a player they *wanted* in free agency, they would *get* him. The question is, *who* did the Marlins, a team early in its construction and far from contention, *want* in free agency? Why *didn't* they want *the best* players? And are they really ready to get *better*?

Because, you know, the Marlins *are* a tanking team, and that means for now, the *best* players available are still invisible to them. So, what have the Marlins gained by spending the last decade as an unwatched franchise under .500? As far as people you know who've put on the famous Midnight Black, Miami Blue, and Caliente Red uniforms, Martin Prado, Curtis Granderson and Neil Walker have been phased out. Wei-Yin Chen's contract is finally disintegrating, and they bought out Starlin Castro's deal.

If you are a Marlins fan, this is very scary! Not because of who these players are, but because of the fun 2019 baseball activity of saying the names of players who aren't on the Marlins anymore: Giancarlo Stanton. Christian Yelich. J.T. Realmuto. Marcell Ozuna. Dee Gordon. For a few weeks at the beginning of 2019, it seemed like it was going to be the Year of Derek Dietrich during which the former Marlins second baseman would do things that no one on the *current* Marlins could do, like hit three home runs in a game and extremely piss off Chris Archer. Dietrich returned to being a random infielder who hits .187 eventually, but for a while, it looked like the best thing that could happen to a major-league ball player in 2019 was to no longer play for the Marlins.

Every plan, whether a meandering franchise rebuild or burning your apartment down and moving into a shack in the local swamp, has a final phase. When will the Marlins reach theirs? If this past winter is any indication, they're still stroking their chins at mid-range free agent options, signing outfielder Corey Dickerson and checking in on Kole Calhoun and Yasiel Puig. They also acquired infielder Jonathan Villar, who instantly went from being the best player on the Orioles to being the best player on the Marlins, via trade. They locked up manager Don Mattingly with an extension, despite a record almost a hundred games under .500 over four years. Whatever you want to see from a manager in his situation, Miami has seen it. Maybe they want an expert on-hand who has experience in shaving a signature mustache and is aware of how effective it was in remaking himself.

Miami Marlins 2020

And there are players *currently* on the team to contribute to their future, more successful persona of their franchise; they just had to cycle through a few identities to get here. The Marlins turned Marcell Ozuna into Zac Gallen and turned Zac Gallen into toolsy prospect, Jazz Chisholm. Now, instead of waiting out another will-he-or-won't-he pitching prospect, the Marlins have a potent, barefooted shortstop of the future. Sandy Alcantara, Caleb Smith and Pablo Lopez are all young pitchers who have had their names mentioned in earnest this past season, with Alcantara and his high-90s fastball serving as Miami's annual obligatory All-Star. Brian Anderson was one of the few pistons firing on the Marlins offense in 2019, and when he came up with the bases loaded against the Phillies on August 23, the hope was that he would improve on his already impressive numbers. Instead, he was hit in the hand with a 93 mph fastball, and his season was over.

As key young players heal, the perception of Jeter, too, is on the mend—that is, if you consider iconic Yankees shortstop Derek Jeter and bumbling Marlins part-owner Derek Jeter the same person. His name being on the Hall of Fame ballot this winter ended the novelty of Jeter-as-owner critiques and reminded writers why they got into this business in the first place: to vote Derek Jeter into the Hall of Fame. In some cases, they intend to do so while voting for absolutely no one else, out of fear of tarnishing Jeter's induction. And just look at the places you can find Jeter in his adopted hometown of Miami: An elementary school. A holiday food drive. Infielder Miguel Rojas bothered to say of Jeter and owner Bruce Sherman, "They are always going to tell you the truth from day one." Finally, some *good* press for the guy, and he didn't even have to remote crash his private jet in the Everglades and start wearing a fake beard.

So there's a little bit going on for the Marlins, but a key part of a rebuild, and of faking your death, is patience. Patience to bide your time. To wait for your moment. To watch things develop until you can resurface. That's asking a lot of everyone involved. And until that time comes, all you can do is hide in the basement while the authorities embark on a fruitless search for your corpse and be sure to never go outside in the same outfit.

The Marlins' scheme to fake their death over the last few years has an ironically fatal flaw: Sure, they've worn two sets of new uniforms and tried to destroy evidence of their existence by dragging the home run sculpture out to the dumpster, but we still know it's them. There are at least a couple of fans waiting for them to resurface—think of them like investigators scrolling through internet searches, formulating theories as to what exactly the Marlins are up to, and watching their every move to see if their theories were correct. The Marlins have got to know how to distract them in the short-term so they can keep changing their long-term appearance.

On September 20, Marlins outfielder Austin Dean threw a ball into the stands and knocked an empty can off the top of a pile of other cans. We can talk about the future all we want, but the team and its dwindling fan base still has to survive the present. Rebuilds are not fun and should not be celebrated, but the team will still exist whether it's making an effort to win or not. There will be players on it and, presumably, the whole mess they've put together will develop a little more in 2020. It may seem like inconsequential social media fodder, but the Marlins will need many, many little moments, like a career minor leaguer sniping a tin can from the grass, to help remind people at a Marlins game that they are still alive. You have to be able to look in the mirror and, though you are now quite altered, still be able to recognize yourself; to see past all of the changes and secrets and lies and know that the team you want to be is still in there, under the tilted brim of a soiled ball cap. Because that's the trick with faking your death—the main part of it, really: You're not actually supposed to die.

—*Justin Klugh is an author of Baseball Prospectus.*

Part 2: Player Analysis

PLAYER COMMENTS WITH GRAPHS

Jesús Aguilar 1B
Born: 06/30/90 Age: 30 Bats: R Throws: R
Height: 6'3" Weight: 250 Origin: International Free Agent, 2007

YEAR	TEAM	LVL	AGE	PA	R	2B	3B	HR	RBI	BB	K	SB	CS	AVG/OBP/SLG
2017	MIL	MLB	27	311	40	15	2	16	52	25	94	0	0	.265/.331/.505
2018	MIL	MLB	28	566	80	25	0	35	108	58	143	0	0	.274/.352/.539
2019	MIL	MLB	29	262	26	9	0	8	34	31	59	0	0	.225/.320/.374
2019	TBA	MLB	29	107	13	3	0	4	16	12	22	0	0	.261/.336/.424
2020	MIA	MLB	30	518	60	21	1	20	66	52	131	1	0	.239/.323/.421

Comparables: Travis Shaw, Brett Wallace, Chris Davis

For the 813rd season in a row, the Rays attempted to buy low on a struggling offensive player that had success the year prior. In 2018, it was Tommy Pham. That worked out really well. In 2019, it was Aguilar. It worked out...less well. An All-Star selection in 2018 when he smashed 60 extra-base hits—including 35 home runs—he collected just seven of them with Tampa Bay after a trade from Milwaukee. Though his exit velocity remained the same, he did not barrel the ball as often and his launch angle dropped nearly three degrees. With three years left until free agency, Aguilar will look to bring the thunder back as the Marlins' starting first baseman.

YEAR	TEAM	LVL	AGE	PA	DRC+	VORP	BABIP	BRR	FRAA	WARP
2017	MIL	MLB	27	311	101	12.4	.337	0.4	1B(77): 1.2, 3B(1): 0.0	0.7
2018	MIL	MLB	28	566	135	35.6	.309	-1.1	1B(132): 3.6, 3B(5): 0.0	3.6
2019	MIL	MLB	29	262	94	2.5	.264	-1.9	1B(60): 0.1, 3B(2): 0.0	0.1
2019	TBA	MLB	29	107	104	2.3	.290	-1.7	1B(15): 0.0	0.1
2020	MIA	MLB	30	518	96	6.5	.290	-1.4	1B 2	0.9

Jesús Aguilar, continued

Batted Ball Distribution

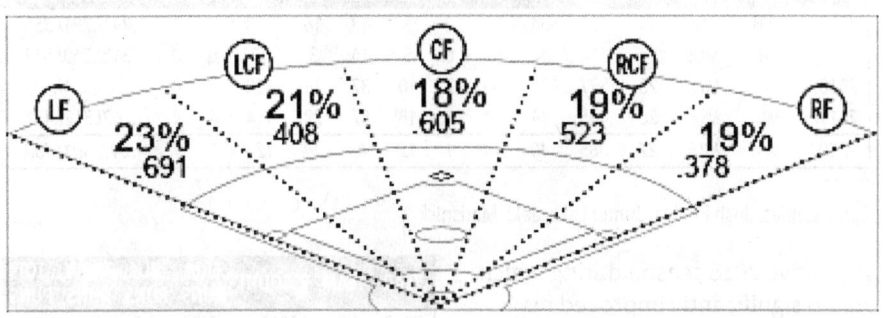

Strike Zone vs LHP **Strike Zone vs RHP**

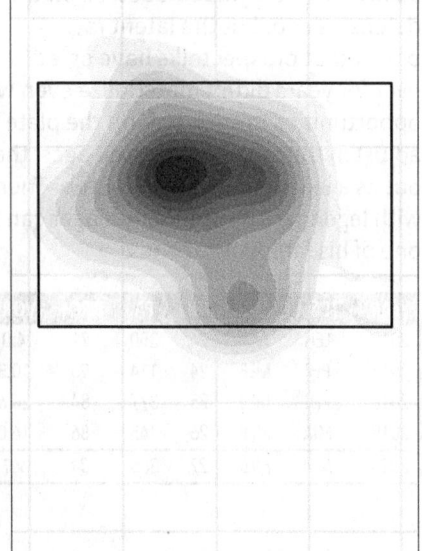

Miami Marlins 2020

Jorge Alfaro C
Born: 06/11/93   Age: 27   Bats: R   Throws: R
Height: 6'2"   Weight: 225   Origin: International Free Agent, 2010

YEAR	TEAM	LVL	AGE	PA	R	2B	3B	HR	RBI	BB	K	SB	CS	AVG/OBP/SLG
2017	LEH	AAA	24	350	34	13	2	7	43	16	113	1	1	.241/.291/.358
2017	PHI	MLB	24	114	12	6	0	5	14	3	33	0	0	.318/.360/.514
2018	PHI	MLB	25	377	35	16	2	10	37	18	138	3	0	.262/.324/.407
2019	MIA	MLB	26	465	44	14	1	18	57	22	154	4	4	.262/.312/.425
2020	MIA	MLB	27	385	40	14	1	12	45	18	126	1	1	.248/.301/.400

Comparables: Josh Phelps, Junior Lake, Jake Marisnick

A positive 2018 season during which Alfaro significantly improved his framing gave way to a somewhat middling 2019, during which he had to catch the illustrious Marlins pitching staff. Alfaro still graded out well on the defensive end, but the latent raw power that prospectniks have ogled over for years didn't materialize even with the juiced ball. He'll have many opportunities to stick behind the plate and garner enough plate appearances to adjust in the majors, but as he ages, the odds only increase that Alfaro will max out as a league-average backstop. Then again, catchers are weird and someone with legendary tools as a teenager can turn into a post-hype darling as fast as one of his fabled pop times.

YEAR	TEAM	P. COUNT	FRM RUNS	BLK RUNS	THRW RUNS	TOT RUNS
2017	LEH	10516	2.0	-0.5	0.3	0.9
2017	PHI	4051	-2.6	0.2	-0.1	-2.9
2018	PHI	14100	12.3	-2.4	0.0	10.2
2019	MIA	16910	-1.7	-3.5	0.1	-5.2
2020	MIA	14686	1.6	-2.9	0.0	-1.2

YEAR	TEAM	LVL	AGE	PA	DRC+	VORP	BABIP	BRR	FRAA	WARP
2017	LEH	AAA	24	350	71	4.0	.345	-1.4	C(77): 4.8	0.9
2017	PHI	MLB	24	114	93	10.3	.420	-1.5	C(28): -2.5, 1B(2): 0.1	0.1
2018	PHI	MLB	25	377	84	24.6	.406	0.5	C(104): 12.2, 3B(1): 0.0	2.5
2019	MIA	MLB	26	465	86	16.0	.364	-2.1	C(118): -2.0, 1B(1): 0.0	1.1
2020	MIA	MLB	27	385	84	9.1	.349	-0.8	C 1	1.0

Jorge Alfaro, continued

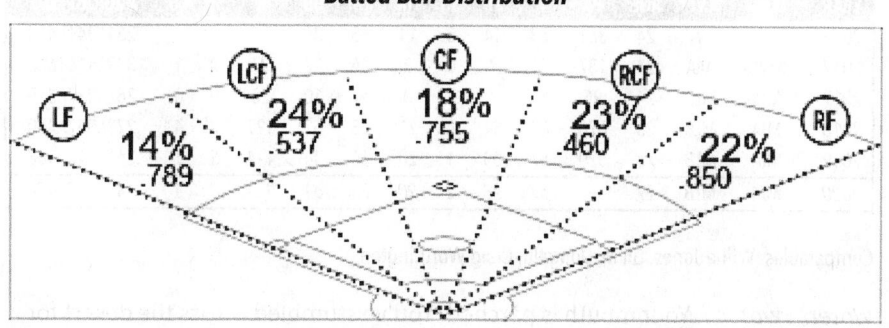

Batted Ball Distribution

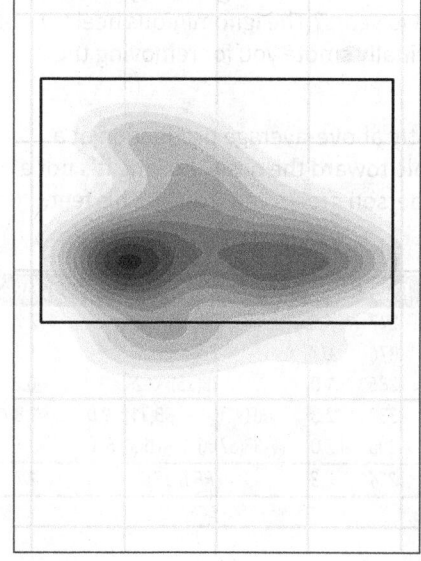

Strike Zone vs LHP

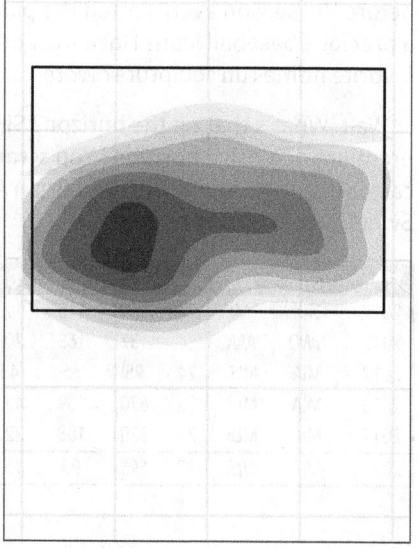

Strike Zone vs RHP

Miami Marlins 2020

Brian Anderson 3B/OF

Born: 05/19/93 Age: 27 Bats: R Throws: R
Height: 6'3" Weight: 185 Origin: Round 3, 2014 Draft (#76 overall)

YEAR	TEAM	LVL	AGE	PA	R	2B	3B	HR	RBI	BB	K	SB	CS	AVG/OBP/SLG
2017	JAX	AA	24	361	53	14	3	14	55	36	71	1	1	.251/.341/.450
2017	NWO	AAA	24	137	21	7	0	8	26	12	27	0	1	.339/.416/.602
2017	MIA	MLB	24	95	11	7	1	0	8	10	28	0	0	.262/.337/.369
2018	MIA	MLB	25	670	87	34	4	11	65	62	129	2	4	.273/.357/.400
2019	MIA	MLB	26	520	57	33	1	20	66	44	114	5	1	.261/.342/.468
2020	MIA	MLB	27	595	67	28	2	20	73	51	131	2	1	.248/.328/.423

Comparables: Willie Jones, Gil McDougald, Craig Worthington

Water... water... Your mouth is parched. You've stumbled across the desert for three days, your canteen's precious few drops long since dried up under the unforgiving sun. *Water...* Three days of sunburn and sand, the hallucinations setting in—you've begun to question yourself, how exactly you got here. What could have damned you to such a fate? Was it the white flag trades you made before the season even started the past two years? The ignominious heel turn of a precious baseball icon? Have the gods finally smote you for removing their favorite home run sculpture? *Water...*

Wait. What's that on the horizon? Slightly above-average production at a premium defensive position? You scramble toward the oasis, praying it's not a cartoon mirage. You arrive, and Brian Anderson greets you. You kiss his feet. Sweet, sweet Brian Anderson.

YEAR	TEAM	LVL	AGE	PA	DRC+	VORP	BABIP	BRR	FRAA	WARP
2017	JAX	AA	24	361	115	19.5	.277	-1.3	3B(82): 9.0	2.7
2017	NWO	AAA	24	137	163	20.4	.376	-0.4	3B(30): 1.5	1.7
2017	MIA	MLB	24	95	66	4.5	.386	1.0	3B(25): -2.2	-0.2
2018	MIA	MLB	25	670	109	43.9	.332	2.3	RF(91): -1.1, 3B(71): -9.0	1.8
2019	MIA	MLB	26	520	108	22.1	.305	2.0	3B(67): 1.1, RF(55): 6.3	3.1
2020	MIA	MLB	27	595	99	15.2	.294	2.3	RF 1, 3B 0	1.7

Brian Anderson, continued

Batted Ball Distribution

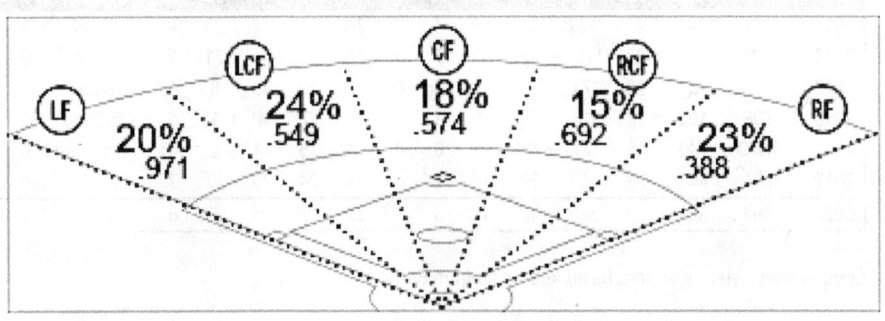

Strike Zone vs LHP   **Strike Zone vs RHP**

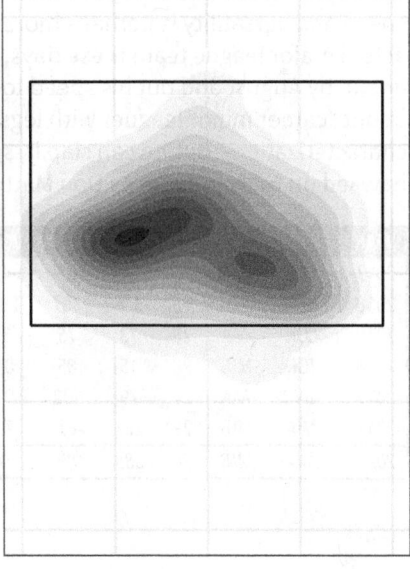

Miami Marlins 2020

Jon Berti UT

Born: 01/22/90   Age: 30   Bats: R   Throws: R
Height: 5'10"   Weight: 195   Origin: Round 18, 2011 Draft (#559 overall)

YEAR	TEAM	LVL	AGE	PA	R	2B	3B	HR	RBI	BB	K	SB	CS	AVG/OBP/SLG
2017	BUF	AAA	27	237	26	8	4	3	20	20	53	23	4	.205/.271/.321
2018	NHP	AA	28	316	55	13	7	8	42	29	46	21	9	.314/.399/.498
2018	COH	AAA	28	73	10	1	0	0	3	9	13	8	1	.217/.333/.233
2018	TOR	MLB	28	15	2	1	1	0	2	0	4	1	0	.267/.267/.467
2019	NWO	AAA	29	79	14	1	0	4	8	15	11	5	0	.290/.430/.500
2019	MIA	MLB	29	287	52	14	1	6	24	24	73	17	3	.273/.348/.406
2020	MIA	MLB	30	385	40	19	3	7	39	32	96	20	6	.253/.328/.388

Comparables: Tyler Ladendorf, David Adams, Quintin Berry

The man who calls himself "Jonny Hustle" (let's hope Berti doesn't get traded to San Diego anytime soon) earned his fins in the final two months of 2019. Seeing time all over the diamond, Berti broke out in a minor mood after spending the better part of the last decade in Toronto's farm system. His combination of speed and versatility is perhaps more attractive to fantasy players than an actual major league team these days, but he nabbed a regular spot in Miami's lineup by August and put his speed to use. Sure, he's scrappy—there's little about "career minor leaguer with legs and glove" that would decry that characterization—but he can slap it, spray it and bop it like an annoying '90s toy hawked on Nickelodeon. As Don Mattingly said, Berti is a "true piece."

YEAR	TEAM	LVL	AGE	PA	DRC+	VORP	BABIP	BRR	FRAA	WARP
2017	BUF	AAA	27	237	62	-4.3	.256	1.9	2B(47): 9.9, LF(13): -0.5	0.9
2018	NHP	AA	28	316	157	28.7	.354	0.6	3B(27): -0.8, 2B(20): -0.1	2.8
2018	COH	AAA	28	73	75	-3.1	.271	-0.5	LF(11): -1.5, 2B(6): -0.2	-0.3
2018	TOR	MLB	28	15	85	0.7	.364	0.6	2B(4): -0.6	0.0
2019	NWO	AAA	29	79	132	9.3	.292	1.2	3B(9): -0.4, CF(6): 1.2	0.8
2019	MIA	MLB	29	287	87	7.3	.360	5.0	SS(32): -1.4, CF(21): -1.2	1.1
2020	MIA	MLB	30	385	89	10.5	.331	2.9	CF -1, SS -1	0.8

Jon Berti, continued

Batted Ball Distribution

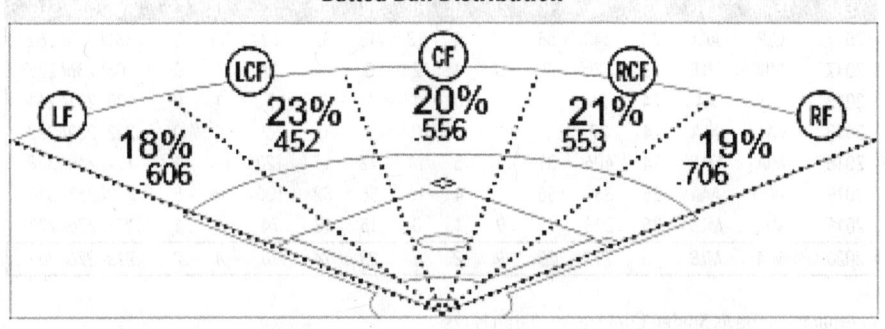

Strike Zone vs LHP **Strike Zone vs RHP**

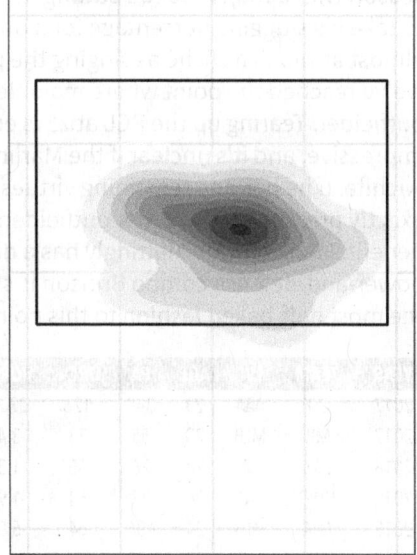

Miami Marlins 2020

Lewis Brinson CF

Born: 05/08/94   Age: 26   Bats: R   Throws: R
Height: 6'3"   Weight: 195   Origin: Round 1, 2012 Draft (#29 overall)

YEAR	TEAM	LVL	AGE	PA	R	2B	3B	HR	RBI	BB	K	SB	CS	AVG/OBP/SLG
2017	CSP	AAA	23	340	66	22	4	13	48	32	62	11	5	.331/.400/.562
2017	MIL	MLB	23	55	2	0	1	2	3	7	17	1	0	.106/.236/.277
2018	JAX	AA	24	26	1	0	0	1	1	3	5	1	0	.130/.231/.261
2018	NWO	AAA	24	27	0	1	1	0	3	0	6	0	0	.222/.222/.333
2018	MIA	MLB	24	406	31	10	5	11	42	17	120	2	1	.199/.240/.338
2019	NWO	AAA	25	339	56	15	4	16	56	32	100	16	5	.270/.361/.510
2019	MIA	MLB	25	248	15	9	1	0	15	13	74	1	1	.173/.236/.221
2020	MIA	MLB	26	217	20	9	2	5	23	14	70	4	2	.213/.276/.362

Comparables: Travis Snider, Clint Frazier, Aaron Hicks

A player with a batting average in the .100s is said to be "on the interstate." Brinson must be going for his learner's permit: He finished his third straight season with a major-league batting average under .200, and he even threatened to take his slugging percentage for a drive. Ranting about Brinson's tools is almost as much a cliché as singing the praises of Joe Kelly's "great stuff," and we've reached the point where major league reps might not help the 25-year-old outfielder. Tearing up the PCL at 25 is encouraging, if not particularly impressive, and it's unclear if the Marlins will be able to develop Brinson in Wichita. If he has any remaining virtues, it's that youth—the Marlins aren't exactly pressed to give other outfielders the reps from which Brinson might benefit. Manager Don Mattingly has a difficult choice to make, though, as the power-and-defense combo Brinson is supposed to possess has manifested in the most half-baked fashion to this point.

YEAR	TEAM	LVL	AGE	PA	DRC+	VORP	BABIP	BRR	FRAA	WARP
2017	CSP	AAA	23	340	126	27.1	.377	1.6	CF(61): 1.1, LF(6): 3.2	2.8
2017	MIL	MLB	23	55	73	-3.4	.107	-0.5	LF(8): -0.1, CF(8): 0.4	0.0
2018	JAX	AA	24	26	55	-1.3	.118	-0.1	CF(8): -1.0	-0.1
2018	NWO	AAA	24	27	64	-1.9	.286	0.0	CF(5): -1.6	-0.2
2018	MIA	MLB	24	406	64	-5.0	.257	-0.9	CF(106): 3.3	-0.1
2019	NWO	AAA	25	339	106	18.7	.356	2.3	CF(49): 4.4, RF(27): 5.1	2.2
2019	MIA	MLB	25	248	42	-1.0	.255	1.5	CF(60): 6.4, RF(11): 0.7	-0.1
2020	MIA	MLB	26	217	64	-2.0	.298	0.0	CF 4	0.2

Lewis Brinson, continued

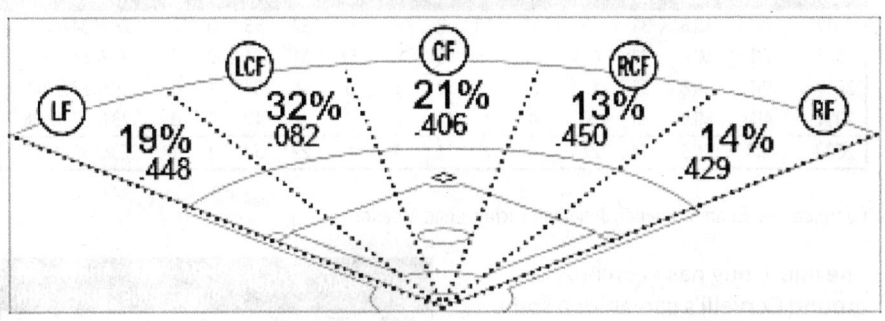

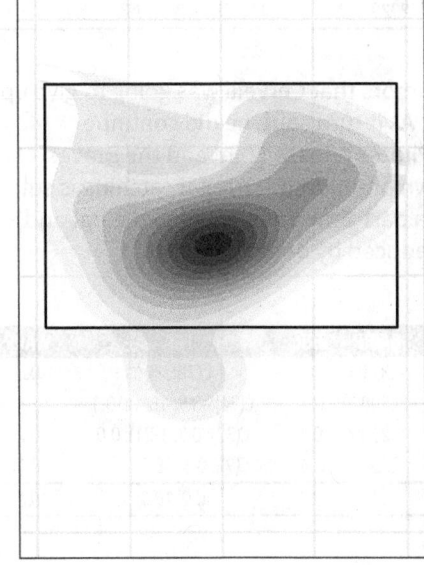

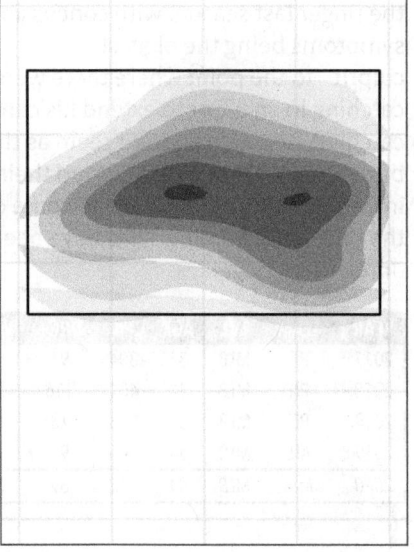

Francisco Cervelli C

Born: 03/06/86   Age: 34   Bats: R   Throws: R
Height: 6'1"   Weight: 210   Origin: International Free Agent, 2003

YEAR	TEAM	LVL	AGE	PA	R	2B	3B	HR	RBI	BB	K	SB	CS	AVG/OBP/SLG
2017	PIT	MLB	31	304	31	13	2	5	31	32	65	0	2	.249/.342/.370
2018	PIT	MLB	32	404	39	15	3	12	57	51	84	2	3	.259/.378/.431
2019	PIT	MLB	33	123	11	3	0	1	5	9	31	1	0	.193/.279/.248
2019	ATL	MLB	33	37	4	5	1	2	7	4	10	0	0	.281/.378/.688
2020	MIA	MLB	34	217	22	8	1	4	21	23	54	1	1	.238/.339/.362

Comparables: Brian Schneider, Jonathan Lucroy, Chad Moeller

The injury bug has been buzzing around Cervelli's career for a some time now, and 2019 was the year when it went from being pesky to a full-on nuisance for the well-regarded catcher. The 34-year-old went through the ringer last season, with concussion symptoms being the biggest culprit—to the point where there were rumors that Cervelli was going to give up catching in an effort to extend his career. As it turns out, he did continue catching, just with another team as the Pirates released him and the Braves brought him on as depth behind their own oft-injured starter. If catching is still in Cervelli's future, it'll have to come on a part-time basis, as both the bat and the once-elite framing skills have been reduced by both age and that unrelenting bug.

YEAR	TEAM	P. COUNT	FRM RUNS	BLK RUNS	THRW RUNS	TOT RUNS
2017	PIT	10368	-6.0	0.5	-1.0	-6.8
2018	PIT	13072	-5.8	-1.1	0.6	-6.5
2019	PIT	4324	0.0	-1.1	0.1	-1.0
2019	ATL	824	0.0	-0.7	0.1	-0.6
2020	MIA	8414	-0.2	-1.2	0.4	-1.1

YEAR	TEAM	LVL	AGE	PA	DRC+	VORP	BABIP	BRR	FRAA	WARP
2017	PIT	MLB	31	304	91	11.7	.311	-2.9	C(78): -5.6	0.3
2018	PIT	MLB	32	404	116	33.7	.308	0.7	C(94): -3.9, 1B(5): -0.1	2.4
2019	PIT	MLB	33	123	73	2.2	.260	-0.3	C(32): 0.3, 1B(1): 0.0	0.2
2019	ATL	MLB	33	37	95	1.4	.350	0.8	C(9): -0.6, 1B(2): -0.1	0.1
2020	MIA	MLB	34	217	89	5.9	.314	-0.1	C 0, 1B 0	0.6

Francisco Cervelli, continued

Batted Ball Distribution

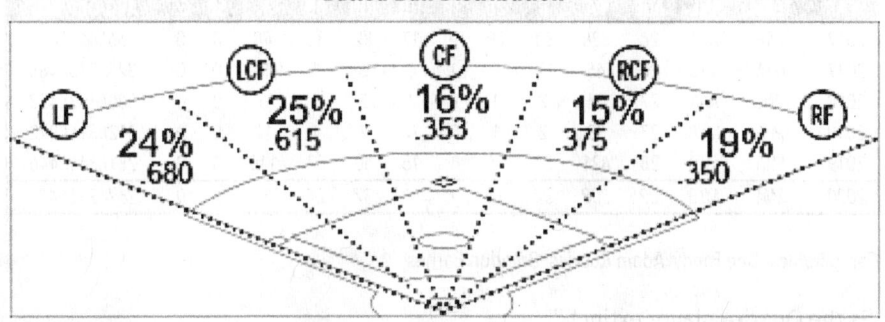

Strike Zone vs LHP **Strike Zone vs RHP**

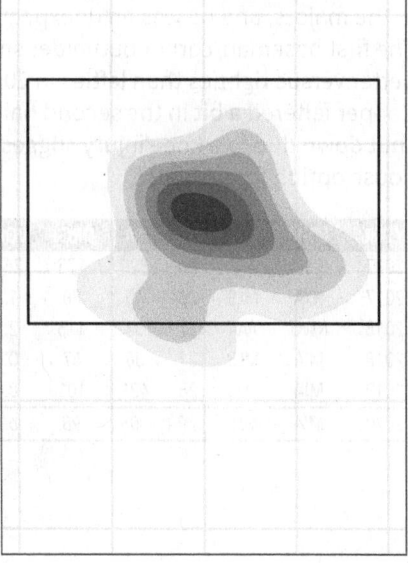

Garrett Cooper   OF/1B

Born: 12/25/90   Age: 29   Bats: R   Throws: R
Height: 6'6"   Weight: 230   Origin: Round 6, 2013 Draft (#182 overall)

YEAR	TEAM	LVL	AGE	PA	R	2B	3B	HR	RBI	BB	K	SB	CS	AVG/OBP/SLG
2017	CSP	AAA	26	320	64	29	0	17	82	33	48	0	0	.366/.428/.652
2017	NYA	MLB	26	45	3	5	1	0	6	1	12	0	0	.326/.333/.488
2018	NWO	AAA	27	34	2	1	0	1	5	3	5	0	0	.300/.382/.433
2018	MIA	MLB	27	38	2	1	0	0	2	4	12	0	0	.212/.316/.242
2019	MIA	MLB	28	421	52	16	1	15	50	33	110	0	0	.281/.344/.446
2020	MIA	MLB	29	308	34	13	1	9	37	24	82	1	0	.267/.331/.421

Comparables: Dee Fondy, Adam Rosales, Brandon Barnes

"Is the Quad-A player extinct?"

The greatest thread in the history of baseball forums, locked after only a few comments because someone remembered Cooper. He mashed in Double-A. He mashed in Triple-A. He's 28 and *thriving*. Cooper's 2019 was his first full season in the majors, and he was an unexpected bright spot for a dismal Marlins club. The first baseman/corner outfielder smokes the ball with regularity and he hit better versus righties than lefties in 2019, despite losing the platoon advantage. Cooper faltered a bit in the second half, but a torrid September before being shut down due to a knee injury suggests that he's currently the Marlins' best in-house option for first base.

YEAR	TEAM	LVL	AGE	PA	DRC+	VORP	BABIP	BRR	FRAA	WARP
2017	CSP	AAA	26	320	173	26.6	.386	-2.3	1B(73): 4.3	3.5
2017	NYA	MLB	26	45	80	1.3	.438	0.0	1B(13): 0.0	0.0
2018	NWO	AAA	27	34	115	2.5	.333	-0.5	1B(5): 0.3, LF(4): 0.5	0.1
2018	MIA	MLB	27	38	67	0.3	.333	0.4	LF(6): 0.7, 1B(4): 1.1	0.1
2019	MIA	MLB	28	421	101	8.4	.357	-0.4	1B(73): -0.2, RF(31): 5.1	1.2
2020	MIA	MLB	29	308	98	6.7	.346	0.0	1B 1, RF 1	0.9

Garrett Cooper, continued

Batted Ball Distribution

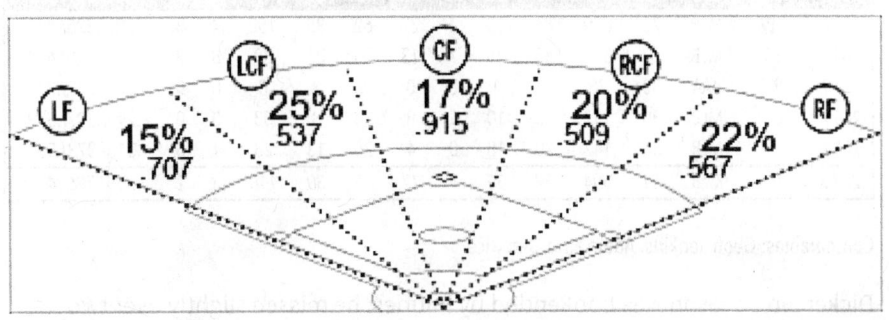

Strike Zone vs LHP	Strike Zone vs RHP

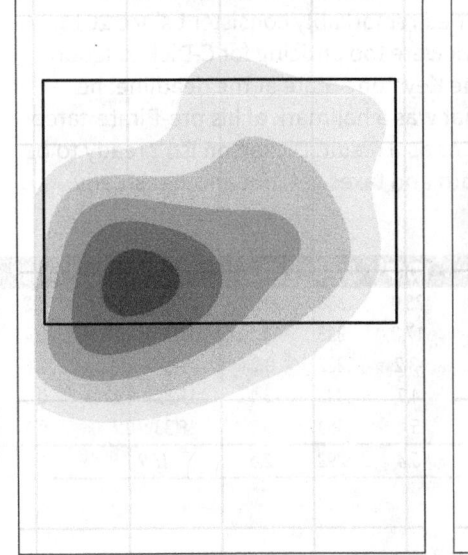 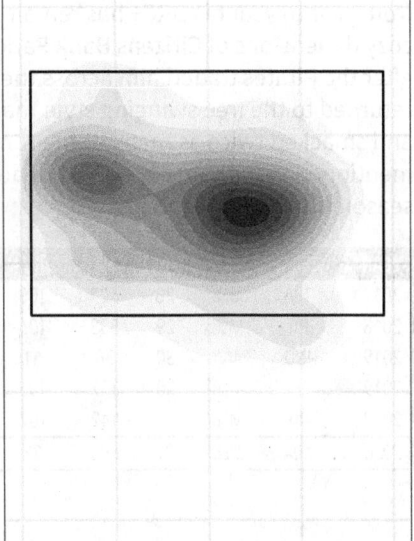

Miami Marlins 2020

Corey Dickerson LF
Born: 05/22/89 Age: 31 Bats: L Throws: R
Height: 6'1" Weight: 210 Origin: Round 8, 2010 Draft (#260 overall)

YEAR	TEAM	LVL	AGE	PA	R	2B	3B	HR	RBI	BB	K	SB	CS	AVG/OBP/SLG
2017	TBA	MLB	28	629	84	33	4	27	62	35	152	4	3	.282/.325/.490
2018	PIT	MLB	29	533	65	35	7	13	55	21	80	8	3	.300/.330/.474
2019	IND	AAA	30	38	4	1	0	0	4	3	8	0	0	.182/.237/.212
2019	PHI	MLB	30	137	13	10	2	8	34	3	33	0	0	.293/.307/.579
2019	PIT	MLB	30	142	20	18	0	4	25	13	23	1	0	.315/.373/.551
2020	MIA	MLB	31	504	52	30	4	17	63	30	110	3	2	.250/.296/.437

Comparables: Geoff Jenkins, Adam Lind, Jim Rice

Dickerson's season was bookended by injuries: he missed slightly over two months of action at the beginning of 2019 with a posterior shoulder strain and ended it with a fractured left foot in mid-September. The meat in between that injury bread was another productive campaign. Dickerson is a slightly above average major league outfielder, and while the shape of his contribution varies from year to year his DRC+ has remained remarkably consistent since 2015. The cozy dimensions of Citizens Bank Park were too enticing for C-Dick to ignore after the Pirates traded him across the Keystone State at the deadline; he returned to the free swinging style that was a hallmark of his pre-Pirate career and smacked twice as many home runs as a result. Dickerson isn't ready to be mentioned in the same breath as death and taxes yet, but another steady season is on the horizon in 2020.

YEAR	TEAM	LVL	AGE	PA	DRC+	VORP	BABIP	BRR	FRAA	WARP
2017	TBA	MLB	28	629	109	25.0	.338	-1.9	LF(93): 13.4	3.2
2018	PIT	MLB	29	533	106	17.2	.333	-4.1	LF(124): 10.7	2.4
2019	IND	AAA	30	38	61	-3.2	.222	0.2	LF(7): 0.6	0.0
2019	PHI	MLB	30	137	105	4.7	.333	-3.1	LF(32): -1.2	0.0
2019	PIT	MLB	30	142	107	5.4	.353	-0.1	LF(33): -0.7	0.5
2020	MIA	MLB	31	504	92	5.4	.292	-2.6	LF 9	1.5

Corey Dickerson, continued

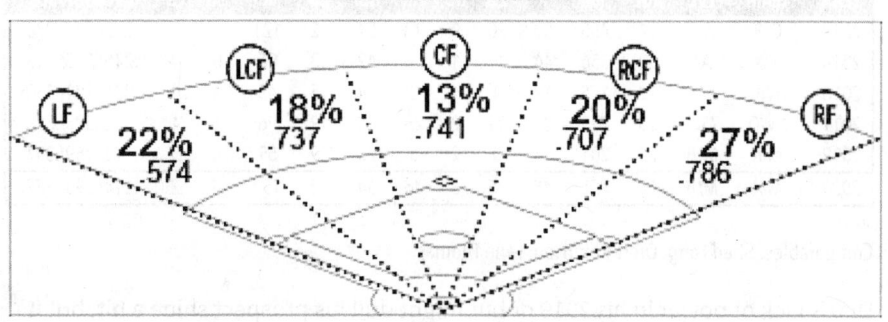

Batted Ball Distribution

Strike Zone vs LHP

Strike Zone vs RHP

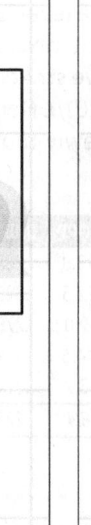
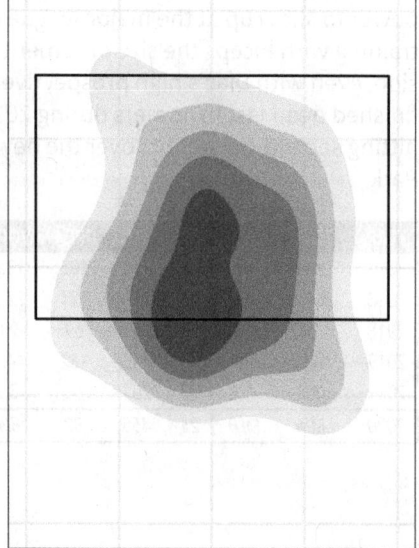

Miami Marlins 2020

Isan Díaz 2B

Born: 05/27/96   Age: 24   Bats: L   Throws: R
Height: 5'10"   Weight: 185   Origin: Round 2, 2014 Draft (#70 overall)

YEAR	TEAM	LVL	AGE	PA	R	2B	3B	HR	RBI	BB	K	SB	CS	AVG/OBP/SLG
2017	CAR	A+	21	455	59	20	0	13	54	62	121	9	3	.222/.334/.376
2018	JAX	AA	22	356	44	19	1	10	42	53	95	10	3	.245/.365/.418
2018	NWO	AAA	22	155	19	4	4	3	14	15	45	4	0	.204/.281/.358
2019	NWO	AAA	23	435	89	21	2	26	70	49	96	5	4	.305/.395/.578
2019	MIA	MLB	23	201	17	5	2	5	23	19	59	0	3	.173/.259/.307
2020	MIA	MLB	24	455	48	18	3	16	54	42	133	4	2	.214/.293/.389

Comparables: Shed Long, Drew Robinson, Lane Thomas

Díaz's lack of power in his 2019 debut might dull his prospect shine a bit, but it really shouldn't. He still wielded a loud bat with authority in the superball-enhanced PCL and walked a ton. Now fully ensconced at second, Díaz is a good bet to fill into a profile not dissimilar to former Fish second-sacker Dan Uggla. The biggest questions for Díaz are whether he'll make enough contact for the power to show up at the major-league level, and if he'll come into spring training with biceps the size of cement mixers. This sort of power from the left side, even with Díaz's high prospective strikeout rate, is appealing to a team that finished dead last in homers during 2019. Here's to Díaz getting ripped and hitting second-deck shots over the newly-moved walls at Pro Player...er, Marlins Park.

YEAR	TEAM	LVL	AGE	PA	DRC+	VORP	BABIP	BRR	FRAA	WARP
2017	CAR	A+	21	455	105	13.8	.283	0.1	2B(70): -1.9, SS(32): -4.8	0.9
2018	JAX	AA	22	356	124	22.5	.325	0.0	2B(82): 2.1	2.2
2018	NWO	AAA	22	155	69	-2.0	.278	0.8	2B(35): -1.6	-0.2
2019	NWO	AAA	23	435	132	44.6	.349	0.7	2B(98): 0.8	3.1
2019	MIA	MLB	23	201	63	-3.2	.224	0.1	2B(48): 0.0	-0.3
2020	MIA	MLB	24	455	82	8.4	.275	1.1	2B 0	0.8

Isan Díaz, continued

Batted Ball Distribution

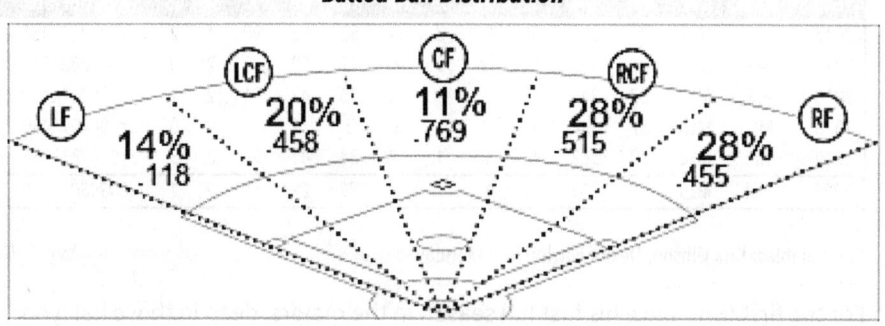

Strike Zone vs LHP **Strike Zone vs RHP**

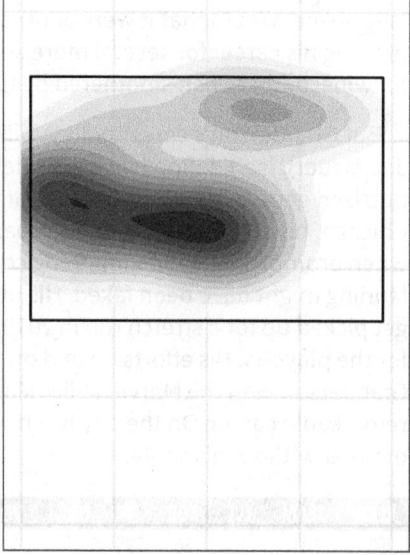

Curtis Granderson LF

Born: 03/16/81 Age: 39 Bats: L Throws: R
Height: 6'1" Weight: 200 Origin: Round 3, 2002 Draft (#80 overall)

YEAR	TEAM	LVL	AGE	PA	R	2B	3B	HR	RBI	BB	K	SB	CS	AVG/OBP/SLG
2017	NYN	MLB	36	395	58	22	3	19	52	53	90	4	2	.228/.334/.481
2017	LAN	MLB	36	132	16	2	0	7	12	18	33	2	0	.161/.288/.366
2018	TOR	MLB	37	349	48	21	1	11	35	42	96	2	1	.245/.342/.430
2018	MIL	MLB	37	54	12	1	1	2	3	12	10	0	0	.220/.407/.439
2019	MIA	MLB	38	363	44	17	1	12	34	41	98	0	3	.183/.281/.356
2020	MIA	MLB	39	251	27	11	1	9	29	29	69	2	1	.203/.303/.379

Comparables: Kirk Gibson, Dexter Fowler, Rick Monday

For the first time since his first full season in the majors, deep in those halcyon mid-2000s now gauzy with the soft light of Remembering Some Guys, Granderson turned in a below-average offensive season while healthy. It's tough to quantify which act of his career this is, but the eminently likable outfielder exhibited some pennant-race savoir faire as recently as his 2018 stint with Milwaukee. Would that it were another era for Mr. Granderson, who might prolong his career for several more seasons if free agency (and many teams' lust for wins) hadn't been smothered by the ownership class.

But Granderson's career twilight, like contemporaries (Ichiro, CC Sabathia, Joe Mauer), isn't defined by his on-field performance. Rather, we remember his outsized generosity: He donated a large sum to the University of Illinois-Chicago, his alma mater, to build a baseball stadium. His idiosyncrasies: In 2015, when prompted to say "something controversial," he posited that the moon landing might have been faked. His obvious love for baseball: While he didn't get picked up for a stretch run in 2019, he did saddle up in the broadcast booth for the playoffs. His efforts on and off the field didn't go unrecognized, either, as Granderson won the Marvin Miller Man of the Year Award four times for his remarkable career. On the day he chooses to retire, the game will be slightly dimmer without his smile.

YEAR	TEAM	LVL	AGE	PA	DRC+	VORP	BABIP	BRR	FRAA	WARP
2017	NYN	MLB	36	395	107	26.0	.251	1.5	CF(59): -8.4, RF(30): 1.9	1.0
2017	LAN	MLB	36	132	107	2.7	.153	0.2	LF(26): -3.2, RF(8): 0.2	0.2
2018	TOR	MLB	37	349	100	8.0	.321	-2.3	LF(41): 0.5, RF(31): -1.9	0.4
2018	MIL	MLB	37	54	100	3.4	.241	-0.5	RF(14): -0.5, LF(3): -0.1	0.0
2019	MIA	MLB	38	363	83	2.5	.220	-1.1	LF(85): 4.7, RF(6): -0.2	0.6
2020	MIA	MLB	39	251	81	1.8	.254	-0.2	LF 1, RF 0	0.1

Curtis Granderson, continued

Batted Ball Distribution

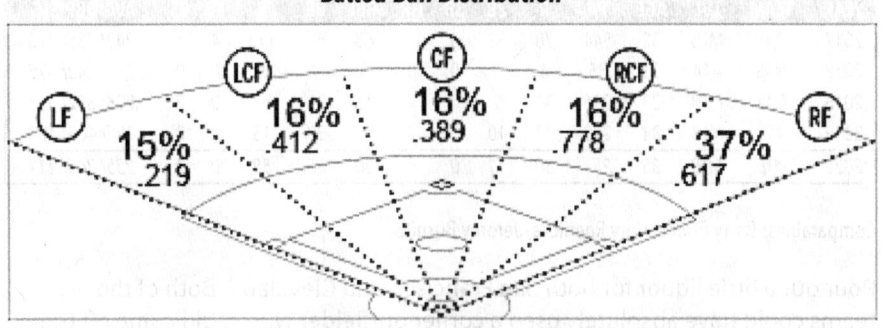

Strike Zone vs LHP   **Strike Zone vs RHP**

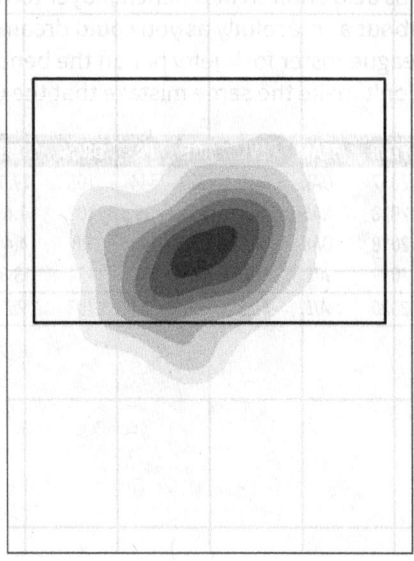

Matt Joyce RF

Born: 08/03/84   Age: 35   Bats: L   Throws: R
Height: 6'2"   Weight: 200   Origin: Round 12, 2005 Draft (#360 overall)

YEAR	TEAM	LVL	AGE	PA	R	2B	3B	HR	RBI	BB	K	SB	CS	AVG/OBP/SLG
2017	OAK	MLB	32	544	78	33	0	25	68	66	113	4	1	.243/.335/.473
2018	NAS	AAA	33	35	4	3	0	0	3	3	5	0	0	.281/.343/.375
2018	OAK	MLB	33	246	34	9	0	7	15	35	53	0	2	.208/.322/.353
2019	ATL	MLB	34	238	32	10	0	7	23	38	45	0	0	.295/.408/.450
2020	ATL	MLB	35	251	30	11	0	9	30	35	58	2	1	.235/.345/.411

Comparables: Barry Bonds, Gary Roenicke, Jeromy Burnitz

Pour out a little liquor for both San Francisco and Cleveland. Both of those teams could have absolutely used a corner outfielder who could come off the bench to provide capable defense and potent offense against right-handed pitching. That's exactly what Joyce ended up giving Atlanta, as the outfielder has now fully embraced his journeyman status at this late stage in his career. He has also entered into bench player territory, though he made that transition about as gracefully as you could dream of. There's always room on a major league roster for a lefty bat off the bench—here's hoping that two more teams don't make the same mistake that the Giants and Indians did.

YEAR	TEAM	LVL	AGE	PA	DRC+	VORP	BABIP	BRR	FRAA	WARP
2017	OAK	MLB	32	544	108	19.0	.263	1.9	RF(115): 0.6, LF(24): 2.4	2.3
2018	NAS	AAA	33	35	102	1.6	.333	-0.3	LF(6): 0.0	0.1
2018	OAK	MLB	33	246	98	4.4	.242	0.1	LF(49): 2.0, RF(6): -0.3	0.7
2019	ATL	MLB	34	238	124	13.8	.351	1.4	RF(33): 0.7, LF(4): -0.6	1.5
2020	ATL	MLB	35	251	103	9.7	.282	0.7	RF 1, LF 1	1.2

Matt Joyce, continued

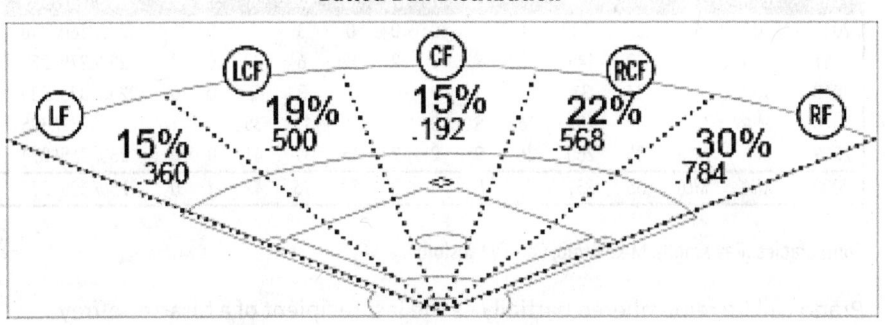

Batted Ball Distribution

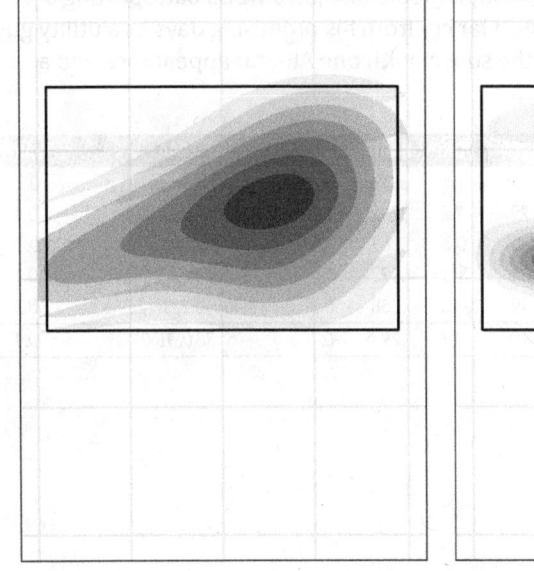

Strike Zone vs LHP

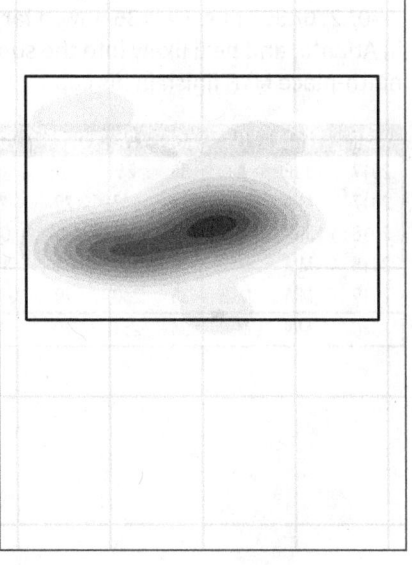

Strike Zone vs RHP

Miami Marlins 2020

Martín Prado CI
Born: 10/27/83 Age: 36 Bats: R Throws: R
Height: 6'0" Weight: 215 Origin: International Free Agent, 2001

YEAR	TEAM	LVL	AGE	PA	R	2B	3B	HR	RBI	BB	K	SB	CS	AVG/OBP/SLG
2017	JUP	A+	33	25	0	1	0	0	0	3	5	0	0	.273/.360/.318
2017	MIA	MLB	33	147	13	9	0	2	12	6	22	0	0	.250/.279/.357
2018	JUP	A+	34	31	3	1	0	0	2	3	2	0	0	.250/.323/.286
2018	MIA	MLB	34	209	16	9	0	1	18	11	35	1	1	.244/.287/.305
2019	MIA	MLB	35	260	26	9	0	2	15	12	41	0	0	.233/.265/.294
2020	MIA	MLB	36	251	22	12	1	3	23	15	42	1	0	.250/.300/.347

Comparables: Ray Knight, Mike Lamb, Carney Lansford

Prado will be remembered partially as the last recipient of a bizarre Jeffrey Loria-blessed contract, one useful for soaking up a bit of payroll if not for acquiring an actually good player. Since signing his three-year extension before the 2017 season, Prado has come to the plate a mere 612 times and hit like he strode up to the plate carrying a pool noodle instead a wood bat, sporting a .240/.276/.308 line. He's 36 now, a far cry from his promising days as a utility guy in Atlanta, and he'll likely into the sunset with one All-Star appearance and a ninth-place MVP finish in his cap.

YEAR	TEAM	LVL	AGE	PA	DRC+	VORP	BABIP	BRR	FRAA	WARP
2017	JUP	A+	33	25	124	1.5	.353	0.2	3B(8): -0.1	0.2
2017	MIA	MLB	33	147	79	-2.3	.282	-1.0	3B(34): -1.2	-0.1
2018	JUP	A+	34	31	116	0.3	.269	0.0	3B(10): 1.2	0.3
2018	MIA	MLB	34	209	84	1.3	.292	0.4	3B(48): -4.5, 1B(1): 0.1	-0.1
2019	MIA	MLB	35	260	70	-3.6	.268	-0.2	1B(40): -0.2, 3B(22): 0.5	-0.3
2020	MIA	MLB	36	251	72	-1.1	.293	-0.1	3B 0, 1B 0	-0.1

Martín Prado, continued

Batted Ball Distribution

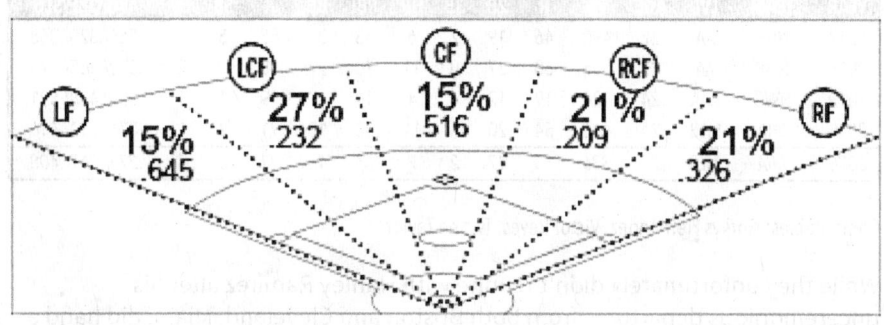

Strike Zone vs LHP   **Strike Zone vs RHP**

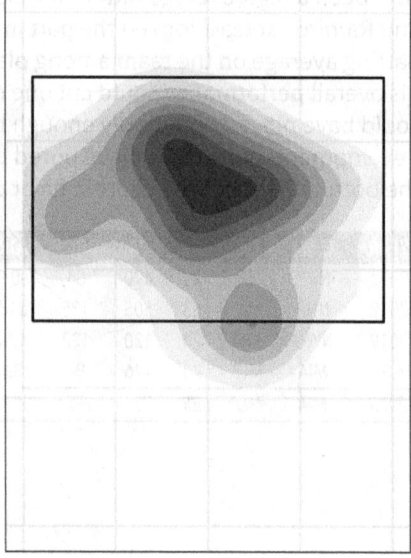

Harold Ramírez OF

Born: 09/06/94   Age: 25   Bats: R   Throws: R
Height: 5'10"   Weight: 220   Origin: International Free Agent, 2011

YEAR	TEAM	LVL	AGE	PA	R	2B	3B	HR	RBI	BB	K	SB	CS	AVG/OBP/SLG
2017	NHP	AA	22	490	46	19	2	6	53	32	65	5	3	.266/.320/.358
2018	NHP	AA	23	505	60	37	0	11	70	27	88	16	2	.320/.365/.471
2019	NWO	AAA	24	120	19	12	1	4	14	6	19	1	1	.355/.408/.591
2019	MIA	MLB	24	446	54	20	3	11	50	18	91	2	1	.276/.312/.416
2020	MIA	MLB	25	336	33	17	2	7	36	16	71	6	3	.274/.319/.408

Comparables: Gorkys Hernández, Victor Reyes, Tyrone Taylor

While they unfortunately didn't reunite with Hanley Ramírez after his unceremonious departures from both Boston and Cleveland, Miami did hand a boatload of plate appearances to a much younger "H. Ramírez." A year removed from an Eastern League playoff MVP award, Ramírez did little to stand out among a crowded Marlins outfield picture while making his major-league debut. He's been a high-average hitter for most of his extensive minor-league career, and Ramírez at least looked the part in that respect, posting the third-highest batting average on the team among players with at least 150 at-bats. However, his overall performance could cut one of two ways with this Miami club: Ramírez could have played acceptably enough to warrant a longer look and some development, or he could have bored the front office enough to find himself at the bottom of the depth chart in favor of some fresher faces with louder tools.

YEAR	TEAM	LVL	AGE	PA	DRC+	VORP	BABIP	BRR	FRAA	WARP
2017	NHP	AA	22	490	84	-0.9	.296	-2.3	RF(73): 0.3, LF(25): -3.4	-0.5
2018	NHP	AA	23	505	135	31.3	.371	2.5	RF(61): -2.7, LF(18): -0.5	2.7
2019	NWO	AAA	24	120	122	12.2	.402	-2.3	LF(16): -0.2, RF(8): 0.1	0.4
2019	MIA	MLB	24	446	84	3.3	.328	-0.2	LF(61): 4.1, RF(55): -2.5	0.7
2020	MIA	MLB	25	336	89	5.6	.334	-0.3	CF 7, LF 1	1.5

Harold Ramirez, continued

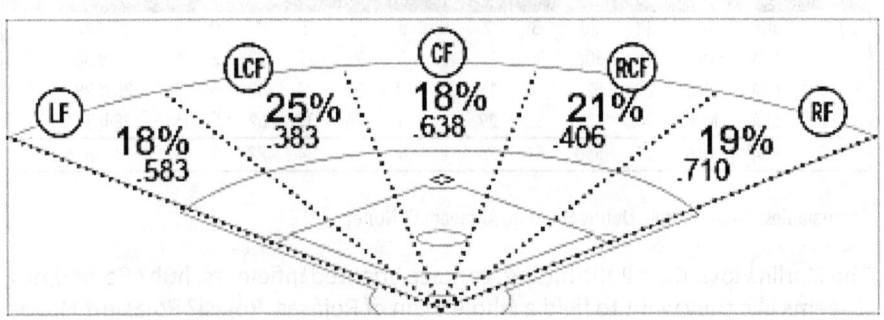

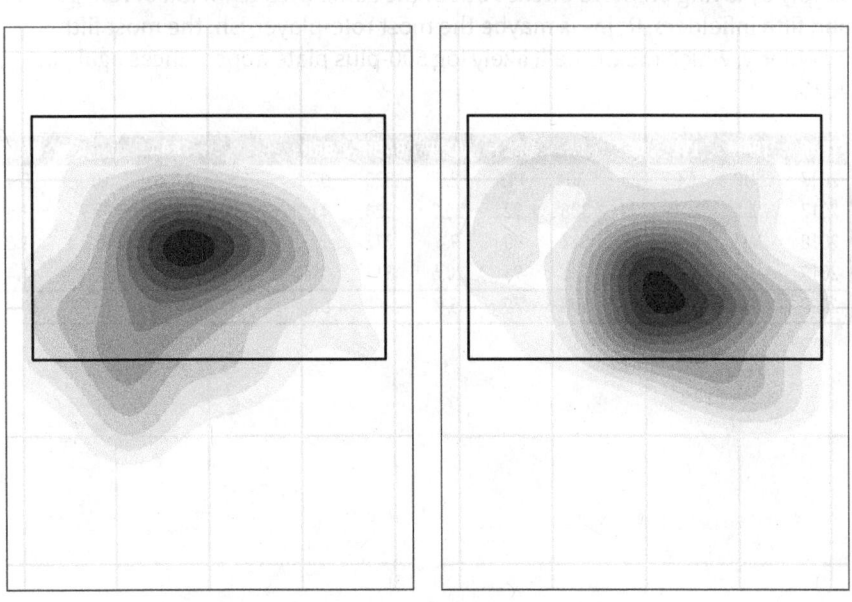

Miami Marlins 2020

Miguel Rojas SS
Born: 02/24/89   Age: 31   Bats: R   Throws: R
Height: 5'11"   Weight: 195   Origin: International Free Agent, 2005

YEAR	TEAM	LVL	AGE	PA	R	2B	3B	HR	RBI	BB	K	SB	CS	AVG/OBP/SLG
2017	JUP	A+	28	30	3	2	0	0	2	3	1	0	1	.308/.400/.385
2017	MIA	MLB	28	306	37	16	2	1	26	27	32	2	1	.290/.361/.375
2018	MIA	MLB	29	527	44	13	0	11	53	24	69	6	3	.252/.297/.346
2019	MIA	MLB	30	526	52	29	1	5	46	32	62	9	5	.284/.331/.379
2020	MIA	MLB	31	560	51	26	2	8	52	34	72	5	3	.263/.316/.364

Comparables: Adam Everett, Denny Hocking, Abraham O. Nunez

The Marlins love their light-hitting, contact-oriented infielders, huh? Sometimes it seems like they want to field a whole team of Rojases. Rojasi? Rojasim? Maybe their plan is to assemble a Manny Alexander Voltron. To his credit, Rojas managed to boost his on-base skills while maintaining a superb contact rate, simply by laying off more pitches out of the zone. On a team full of role players and fifth infielders, Rojas is maybe the most role-player-ish, the most fifth-infielder-y, which means he'll likely log 500-plus plate appearances again in 2020.

YEAR	TEAM	LVL	AGE	PA	DRC+	VORP	BABIP	BRR	FRAA	WARP
2017	JUP	A+	28	30	143	2.7	.320	0.3	2B(3): -0.4, SS(2): 0.0	0.3
2017	MIA	MLB	28	306	92	20.9	.324	4.6	SS(77): -0.2, 3B(15): -0.2	1.5
2018	MIA	MLB	29	527	90	9.1	.272	-2.5	SS(83): 5.4, 1B(49): -0.3	1.6
2019	MIA	MLB	30	526	93	20.6	.314	-1.7	SS(125): -4.8, 1B(6): -0.1	1.4
2020	MIA	MLB	31	560	79	5.9	.293	0.1	SS 1, 2B 0	0.7

Miguel Rojas, continued

Batted Ball Distribution

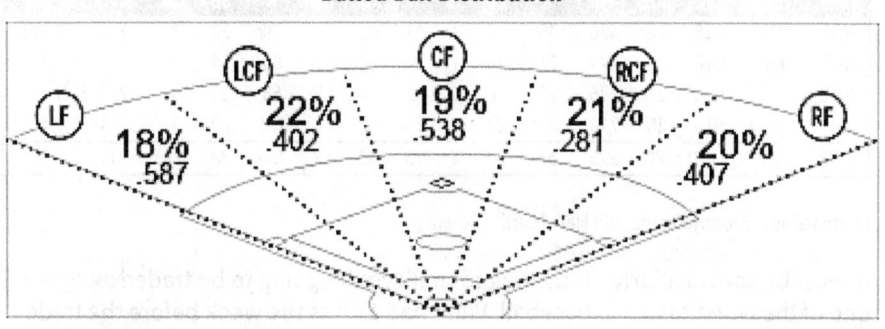

Strike Zone vs LHP

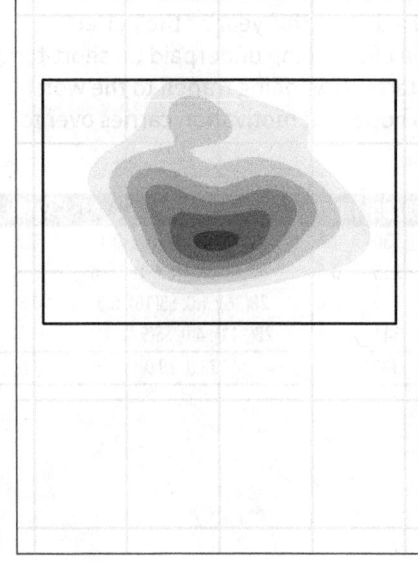

Strike Zone vs RHP

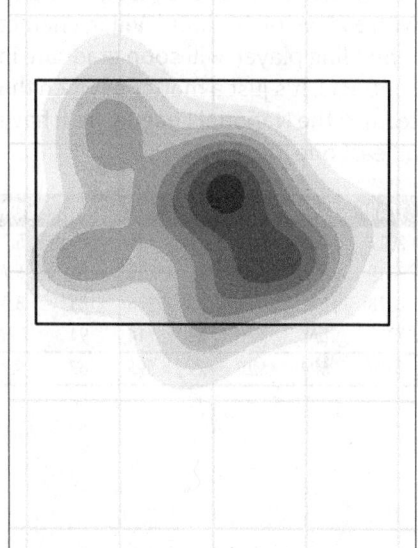

Jonathan Villar MI

Born: 05/02/91   Age: 29   Bats: B   Throws: R
Height: 6'1"   Weight: 215   Origin: International Free Agent, 2008

YEAR	TEAM	LVL	AGE	PA	R	2B	3B	HR	RBI	BB	K	SB	CS	AVG/OBP/SLG
2017	MIL	MLB	26	436	49	18	1	11	40	30	132	23	8	.241/.293/.372
2018	MIL	MLB	27	279	26	10	1	6	22	19	80	14	2	.261/.315/.377
2018	BAL	MLB	27	236	28	4	0	8	24	22	58	21	3	.258/.336/.392
2019	BAL	MLB	28	714	111	33	5	24	73	61	176	40	9	.274/.339/.453
2020	MIA	MLB	29	595	64	23	4	15	63	52	158	38	11	.245/.315/.386

Comparables: Jhonny Peralta, Bill Hall, Everth Cabrera

It must be spectacularly motivating to think you're going to be traded away from one of the worst teams in baseball. Villar had 13 hits the week before the trade deadline, yet he ultimately stayed put. To his credit, he not only kept the party going, but shelved the act where he played like the squirrel in "Ice Age" in favor of a more focused game. That leaves a player who can be utterly dynamic, both on the bases and at the plate, though the perception is better than the reality with a glove on his hand. Villar, characterized aptly this year as the perfect rebuilding player, will soon graduate into a life of being underpaid on short-term contracts. It's just a matter of when that starts. After being traded to the worst team in the National League, he'll have to hope that motivation carries over to at least one more July.

YEAR	TEAM	LVL	AGE	PA	DRC+	VORP	BABIP	BRR	FRAA	WARP
2017	MIL	MLB	26	436	64	5.2	.330	1.6	2B(98): 2.7, CF(6): -0.1	-0.2
2018	MIL	MLB	27	279	82	6.7	.355	0.5	2B(74): -6.1	-0.3
2018	BAL	MLB	27	236	85	8.0	.319	2.4	2B(36): 1.0, SS(18): 0.5	0.8
2019	BAL	MLB	28	714	94	23.6	.341	5.6	2B(111): 4.0, SS(97): 0.9	3.3
2020	MIA	MLB	29	595	87	9.7	.320	2.0	3B 0, 2B 0	1.0

Jonathan Villar, continued

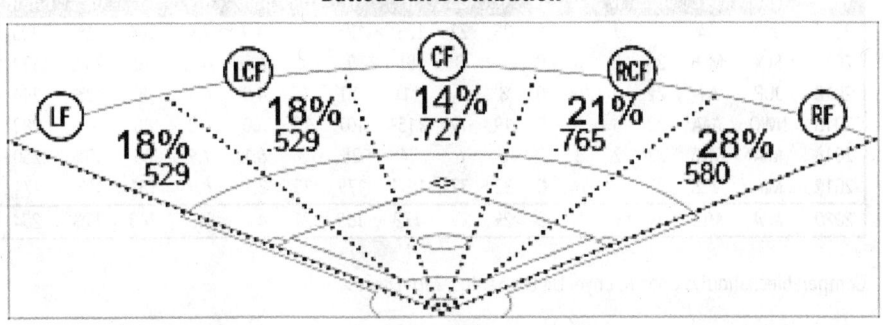

Strike Zone vs LHP   **Strike Zone vs RHP**

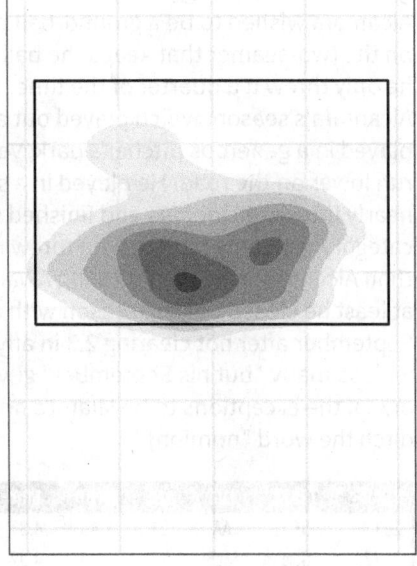

Sandy Alcantara   RHP

Born: 09/07/95   Age: 24   Bats: R   Throws: R
Height: 6'4"   Weight: 170   Origin: International Free Agent, 2013

YEAR	TEAM	LVL	AGE	W	L	SV	G	GS	IP	H	HR	BB/9	K/9	K	GB%	BABIP
2017	SFD	AA	21	7	5	0	25	22	125^1	125	13	3.9	7.6	106	46%	.305
2017	SLN	MLB	21	0	0	0	8	0	8^1	9	2	6.5	10.8	10	26%	.333
2018	JUP	A+	22	0	0	0	3	3	11^1	10	0	4.0	6.4	8	62%	.294
2018	NWO	AAA	22	6	3	0	19	19	115^2	107	10	3.0	6.8	88	50%	.283
2018	MIA	MLB	22	2	3	0	6	6	34	25	3	6.1	7.9	30	50%	.250
2019	MIA	MLB	23	6	14	0	32	32	197^1	179	23	3.7	6.9	151	46%	.271
2020	MIA	MLB	24	9	11	0	29	29	172	163	21	4.0	7.5	143	45%	.284

Comparables: Jhoulys Chacín, Enyel De Los Santos, Zach Davies

Alcantara is a poster child for the high spin rate fastball, and in his first full season in the majors, he sank and ran that devastating pitch to some actual success. He throws his two- and four-seam flavors with sink, and while they generate some swings and misses, the ball-in-play results are disparate. If Alcantara wished to be a ground-ball pitcher in the juiced ball era, he could rely on the two-seamer that keeps the ball on the ground 60 percent of the time—yet he only threw it a quarter of the time. It wasn't the only unusual thing about Alcantara's season, which played out as a litany of nearly-fun fun facts. He played in a generous pitcher's park, yet his ERA at home was three-quarters of a run lower on the road. He played in a season full of increasing reliever usage, yet nearly threw 200 innings and finished seventh in the National League in the bulk category. The only pitcher who threw more innings and gave up fewer homers than Alcantara won the Cy Young Award. Yes, the walks are still concerning but at least he closed out the season with a strikeout-to-walk rate of 3.9 in September after not clearing 2.3 in any other month. Baseball history is littered with so many "but his September" guys though Alcantara doesn't need to be one of the exceptions to be Miami's nominal ace in 2020 - unless he wants to ditch the word "nominal."

YEAR	TEAM	LVL	AGE	WHIP	ERA	DRA	WARP	MPH	FB%	WHF	CSP
2017	SFD	AA	21	1.43	4.31	5.14	0.0				
2017	SLN	MLB	21	1.80	4.32	6.58	-0.1	100.5	66.5	16.8	44.3
2018	JUP	A+	22	1.32	3.97	4.15	0.2				
2018	NWO	AAA	22	1.25	3.89	3.80	2.3				
2018	MIA	MLB	22	1.41	3.44	5.57	-0.1	98.4	60	11.8	45.2
2019	MIA	MLB	23	1.32	3.88	4.56	2.6	97.9	57	11.7	48.7
2020	MIA	MLB	24	1.39	4.23	4.39	2.7	97.8	59.3	12.2	47.8

Sandy Alcantara, continued

Pitch Shape vs LHH	Pitch Shape vs RHH
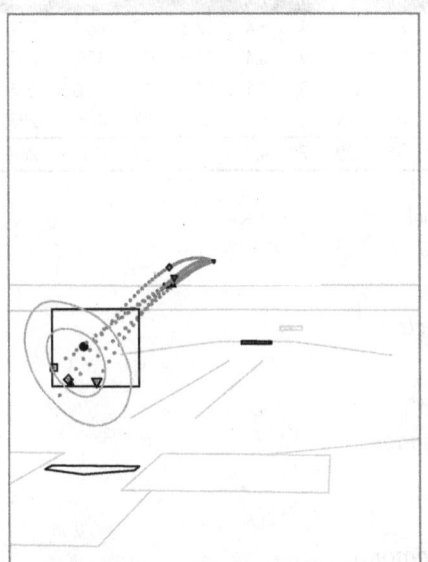	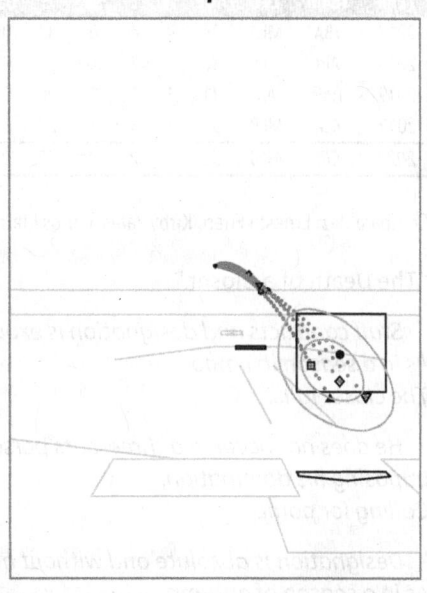

Type	Frequency	Velocity	H Movement	V Movement
● Fastball	29.7%	95.9 [110]	-7.7 [96]	-13.8 [106]
☐ Sinker	27.3%	95.7 [116]	-14.6 [87]	-19.9 [102]
+ Cutter				
▲ Changeup	12.9%	89.6 [116]	-13.8 [88]	-26.8 [102]
✕ Splitter				
▽ Slider	23.6%	86.1 [107]	4.2 [97]	-32.4 [102]
◇ Curveball	6.5%	81.4 [109]	5.3 [91]	-41.7 [112]
✦ Slow Curveball				
✱ Knuckleball				
▼ Screwball				

Brad Boxberger   RHP

Born: 05/27/88   Age: 32   Bats: R   Throws: R
Height: 6'2"   Weight: 205   Origin: Round 1, 2009 Draft (#43 overall)

YEAR	TEAM	LVL	AGE	W	L	SV	G	GS	IP	H	HR	BB/9	K/9	K	GB%	BABIP
2017	TBA	MLB	29	4	4	0	30	0	29^1	23	4	3.4	12.3	40	46%	.292
2018	ARI	MLB	30	3	7	32	60	0	53^1	44	9	5.4	12.0	71	48%	.287
2019	HAR	AA	31	1	1	1	8	0	8^2	6	0	3.1	11.4	11	38%	.286
2019	KCA	MLB	31	1	3	1	29	0	26^2	25	3	5.7	9.1	27	40%	.297
2020	CIN	MLB	32	2	2	0	33	0	35	30	7	4.3	9.9	38	39%	.268

Comparables: Ernesto Frieri, Kirby Yates, Carlos Marmol

"The Death of a Closer."

   Stuff contracts and designation is expected,
As in a season in limbo.
The closer falls.

   He does not become a three-outs personage,
Imposing his domination,
Calling for pomp.

   Designation is absolute and without memorial,
As in a season of autumn,
When the wind stops,

   When the wind stops and, over the heavens,
The dingers go, nevertheless,
In their direction.

YEAR	TEAM	LVL	AGE	WHIP	ERA	DRA	WARP	MPH	FB%	WHF	CSP
2017	TBA	MLB	29	1.16	3.38	2.89	0.7	94.6	65.6	14.3	49.4
2018	ARI	MLB	30	1.42	4.39	5.11	-0.1	93.8	66.3	11.5	46.7
2019	HAR	AA	31	1.04	1.04	3.48	0.1				
2019	KCA	MLB	31	1.58	5.40	6.17	-0.2	92.2	47	12.9	45.6
2020	CIN	MLB	32	1.34	4.36	4.51	0.3	92.5	59.6	12.4	46.5

Brad Boxberger, continued

Pitch Shape vs LHH	Pitch Shape vs RHH
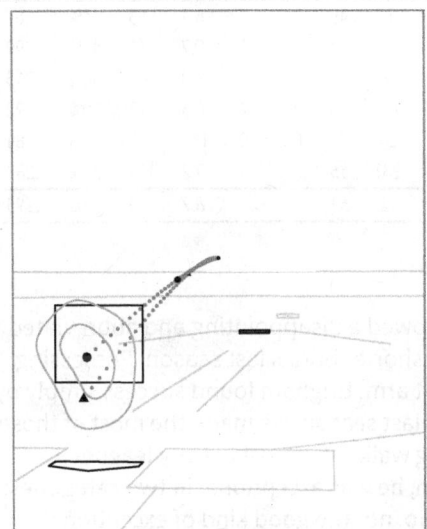	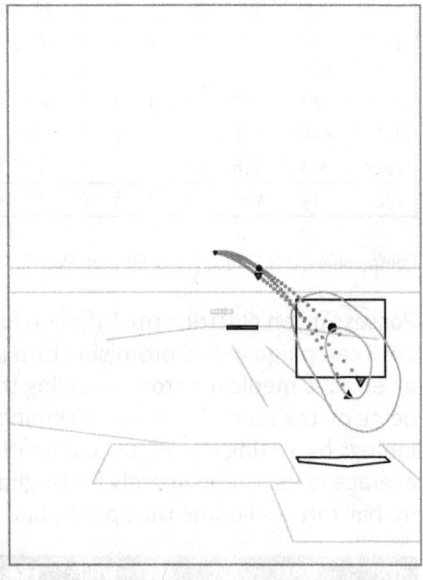

Type	Frequency	Velocity	H Movement	V Movement
● Fastball	47.0%	90.7 [95]	-4.6 [110]	-16.9 [98]
☐ Sinker				
+ Cutter				
▲ Changeup	33.1%	78.9 [77]	-12 [96]	-37 [72]
✗ Splitter				
▽ Slider	19.9%	86.2 [107]	3.9 [95]	-25.8 [121]
◇ Curveball				
⊕ Slow Curveball				
✳ Knuckleball				
▼ Screwball				

Miami Marlins 2020

Jeff Brigham RHP
Born: 02/16/92   Age: 28   Bats: R   Throws: R
Height: 6'0"   Weight: 200   Origin: Round 4, 2014 Draft (#129 overall)

YEAR	TEAM	LVL	AGE	W	L	SV	G	GS	IP	H	HR	BB/9	K/9	K	GB%	BABIP
2017	JUP	A+	25	4	2	0	11	11	59	49	2	3.1	8.1	53	44%	.287
2018	JAX	AA	26	4	1	0	7	7	38	27	1	2.1	9.7	41	41%	.299
2018	NWO	AAA	26	5	2	0	9	9	52^1	53	7	2.2	8.3	48	30%	.315
2018	MIA	MLB	26	0	4	0	4	4	16^1	16	2	7.2	6.6	12	20%	.292
2019	NWO	AAA	27	0	1	2	17	0	24	9	0	3.0	11.2	30	43%	.184
2019	MIA	MLB	27	3	2	1	32	0	38^1	36	8	3.3	9.2	39	34%	.283
2020	MIA	MLB	28	2	3	0	49	0	52	51	9	3.3	8.7	50	33%	.295

Comparables: Luis Santos, Brock Stewart, Ryan Tepera

Possessing an electric arm, Brigham followed a disappointing and abbreviated 2018 campaign with a promising turn in shorter bursts last season. Possessing an eclectic medical history involving that arm, Brigham found success simply by being on the bump for nearly 40 innings last season. He made the most of those innings by getting strikeouts and limiting walks at almost exactly league-average rates. Unfortunately for Brigham, he was exceptional in two categories: fly-ball rate and home runs per fly ball. No, not the good kind of exceptional.

YEAR	TEAM	LVL	AGE	WHIP	ERA	DRA	WARP	MPH	FB%	WHF	CSP
2017	JUP	A+	25	1.17	2.90	3.93	0.9				
2018	JAX	AA	26	0.95	1.18	2.84	1.1				
2018	NWO	AAA	26	1.26	3.44	4.90	0.4				
2018	MIA	MLB	26	1.78	6.06	7.19	-0.4	95.2	61.1	8.9	47.4
2019	NWO	AAA	27	0.71	1.50	1.00	1.2				
2019	MIA	MLB	27	1.30	4.46	4.73	0.3	98.1	51.5	12.3	49.8
2020	MIA	MLB	28	1.35	4.52	4.74	0.4	96.8	54.4	11.5	49

Jeff Brigham, continued

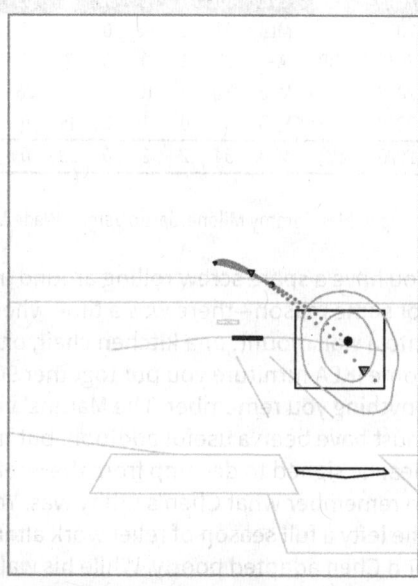

Type	Frequency	Velocity	H Movement	V Movement
● Fastball	51.5%	96.9 [113]	-10.4 [84]	-11.5 [112]
☐ Sinker				
+ Cutter				
▲ Changeup				
✕ Splitter				
▽ Slider	48.5%	83.2 [95]	15.6 [144]	-37.1 [88]
◇ Curveball				
✦ Slow Curveball				
✱ Knuckleball				
▼ Screwball				

Miami Marlins 2020

Wei-Yin Chen LHP
Born: 07/21/85   Age: 34   Bats: R   Throws: L
Height: 6'0"   Weight: 200   Origin: International Free Agent, 2012

YEAR	TEAM	LVL	AGE	W	L	SV	G	GS	IP	H	HR	BB/9	K/9	K	GB%	BABIP
2017	MIA	MLB	31	2	1	0	9	5	33	25	3	2.5	6.8	25	39%	.234
2018	JUP	A+	32	1	0	0	2	2	7^2	5	0	1.2	12.9	11	39%	.278
2018	MIA	MLB	32	6	12	0	26	26	133^1	131	19	3.2	7.5	111	38%	.285
2019	MIA	MLB	33	0	1	0	45	0	68^1	87	15	2.4	8.3	63	38%	.350
2020	MIA	MLB	34	2	2	0	33	0	35	37	7	2.3	7.4	29	38%	.295

Comparables: Tommy Milone, Jason Vargas, Wade Miley

You have a spare screw rolling around in your junk drawer. You know you kept it for some reason—there was a time when it went to something, right? Maybe it fit into a wall mount, or a kitchen chair, or...aw hell, it was probably a spare from some IKEA furniture you put together 90 percent correctly. It doesn't seem to fit anything you remember. The Marlins' vestigial screw is Chen. At one point, he must have been a useful addition, but heading into the final year of a five-year deal he signed to decamp from the wretched Baltimore pitching staff, it's hard to remember what Chen's utility was. Year Four of the regrettable contract gifted the lefty a full season of relief work after working as a starter almost exclusively, and Chen adapted poorly. While his walk and strikeout rates were perfectly cromulent for a Marlins pitcher, Chen gave up a ton of hits, and most of those hits were loud. Even louder still was the slam of the metal doors behind him, as the Marlins unceremoniously dumped Chen and his $22 million in guaranteed money, preventing him from screwing them any further in Year Five.

YEAR	TEAM	LVL	AGE	WHIP	ERA	DRA	WARP	MPH	FB%	WHF	CSP
2017	MIA	MLB	31	1.03	3.82	4.28	0.5	92.8	65	9.5	48.5
2018	JUP	A+	32	0.78	1.17	2.42	0.3				
2018	MIA	MLB	32	1.34	4.79	4.88	0.7	93.4	55.9	9.2	49.1
2019	MIA	MLB	33	1.54	6.59	6.36	-0.7	93.5	50.9	10.2	52.2
2020	MIA	MLB	34	1.31	4.50	4.82	0.2	92.3	54.1	9.4	49.5

Wei-Yin Chen, continued

Pitch Shape vs LHH

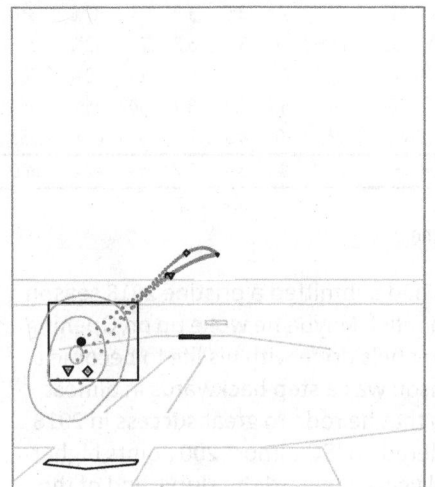

Pitch Shape vs RHH

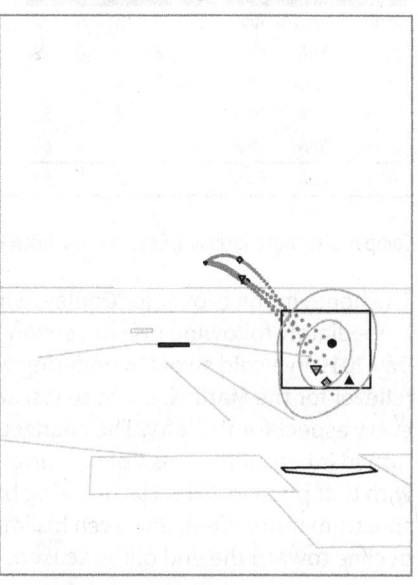

Type	Frequency	Velocity	H Movement	V Movement
● Fastball	48.0%	91.8 [98]	3.4 [115]	-14.4 [104]
□ Sinker				
+ Cutter				
▲ Changeup	3.8%	84.4 [97]	7.4 [117]	-24.6 [108]
✕ Splitter				
▽ Slider	22.8%	86.2 [108]	-4.4 [97]	-26.8 [118]
◇ Curveball	22.4%	74.4 [86]	-6.5 [96]	-55 [84]
⊕ Slow Curveball				
✳ Knuckleball				
▼ Screwball				

Adam Conley   LHP

Born: 05/24/90   Age: 30   Bats: L   Throws: L
Height: 6'3"   Weight: 200   Origin: Round 2, 2011 Draft (#72 overall)

YEAR	TEAM	LVL	AGE	W	L	SV	G	GS	IP	H	HR	BB/9	K/9	K	GB%	BABIP
2017	NWO	AAA	27	3	3	0	12	12	62^1	69	7	3.6	5.9	41	39%	.310
2017	MIA	MLB	27	8	8	0	22	20	102^2	114	19	3.7	6.3	72	42%	.295
2018	NWO	AAA	28	2	4	0	8	8	40	45	6	3.2	5.6	25	50%	.300
2018	MIA	MLB	28	3	4	3	52	0	50^2	37	5	3.2	8.9	50	45%	.250
2019	MIA	MLB	29	2	11	2	60	0	60^2	76	10	4.3	7.9	53	40%	.353
2020	MIA	MLB	30	3	3	2	54	0	58	57	8	3.5	8.2	53	42%	.300

Comparables: Mike Kickham, César Ramos, Brian Flynn

The honeymoon is over for Conley, who had submitted a pristine 2018 season immediately following his conversion to relief. Maybe he woke up on Opening Day 2019 in a cold sweat, wondering what he's done with his life to become a reliever for the Marlins, because last season was a step backwards in almost every aspect for the lefty. The changeup that he rode to great success in 2018 turned into a clunker, as Conley surrendered an ISO almost 200 points higher with that pitch in 2019. His breaking ball veered toward the slurvy end of the spectrum more often, and even his improved fastball showed signs of velocity decline toward the end of the season.

YEAR	TEAM	LVL	AGE	WHIP	ERA	DRA	WARP	MPH	FB%	WHF	CSP
2017	NWO	AAA	27	1.51	5.49	5.79	-0.1				
2017	MIA	MLB	27	1.52	6.14	6.64	-1.2	92.2	64.4	10.6	47.7
2018	NWO	AAA	28	1.48	5.18	5.15	0.2				
2018	MIA	MLB	28	1.09	4.09	3.58	0.8	97.6	56.9	15.6	46.9
2019	MIA	MLB	29	1.73	6.53	6.87	-1.0	97.7	61.7	11.5	51
2020	MIA	MLB	30	1.38	4.30	4.47	0.6	94.8	61.4	12	48.7

Adam Conley, continued

Pitch Shape vs LHH	Pitch Shape vs RHH
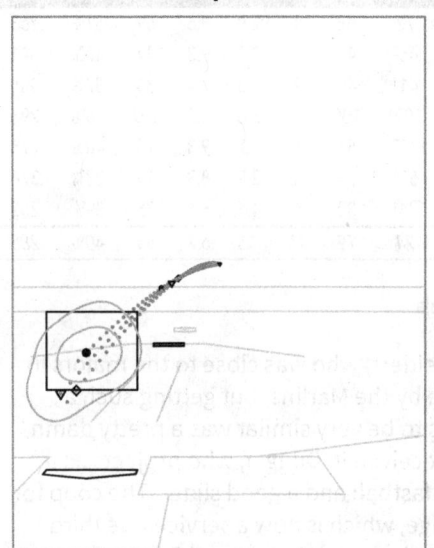	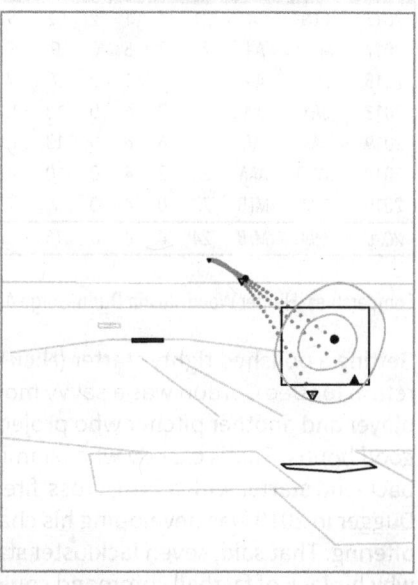

Type	Frequency	Velocity	H Movement	V Movement
● Fastball	61.6%	95.7 [109]	12.2 [76]	-14.7 [103]
☐ Sinker				
+ Cutter				
▲ Changeup	16.8%	86.9 [106]	14.8 [83]	-24.8 [108]
✕ Splitter				
▽ Slider	16.5%	85.9 [107]	-1.8 [86]	-32.7 [101]
◇ Curveball	5.0%	83.3 [115]	-3.2 [83]	-38.4 [119]
⊕ Slow Curveball				
✱ Knuckleball				
▼ Screwball				

Robert Dugger RHP

Born: 07/03/95 Age: 24 Bats: R Throws: R
Height: 6'2" Weight: 180 Origin: Round 18, 2016 Draft (#537 overall)

YEAR	TEAM	LVL	AGE	W	L	SV	G	GS	IP	H	HR	BB/9	K/9	K	GB%	BABIP
2017	CLN	A	21	4	1	2	22	9	72	55	4	2.0	8.6	69	51%	.263
2017	MOD	A+	21	2	5	0	9	9	45^2	49	4	3.2	9.3	47	40%	.341
2018	JUP	A+	22	3	1	0	7	7	41^1	40	2	1.5	7.4	34	57%	.306
2018	JAX	AA	22	7	6	0	18	18	109^1	100	13	3.0	8.8	107	36%	.296
2019	JAX	AA	23	6	6	0	13	13	70^2	57	6	2.7	9.3	73	48%	.276
2019	NWO	AAA	23	2	4	0	10	10	53^1	74	12	2.9	8.3	49	38%	.376
2019	MIA	MLB	23	0	4	0	7	7	34^1	33	6	4.5	6.6	25	39%	.262
2020	MIA	MLB	24	4	6	0	15	15	74	79	15	3.5	6.7	55	40%	.285

Comparables: Hunter Wood, Justin Dunn, Jorge Alcala

Getting a polished righty starter (Nick Neidert) who was close to the majors in return for Dee Gordon was a savvy move by the Marlins, but getting such a player and another pitcher who projects to be very similar was a pretty damn good bonus. That's exactly who Miami received in Dugger, who projects as a back-end starter with a firm, cross-fired fastball and a good slider. The coup for Dugger in 2019 was developing his change, which is now a serviceable third offering. That said, seven lackluster starts between August and September show why his lack of fastball command could be enough to condemn him to relief. Still, the stuff is there, and he's only 24. Add him to the list of potential role-5 arms in the Marlins' stable.

YEAR	TEAM	LVL	AGE	WHIP	ERA	DRA	WARP	MPH	FB%	WHF	CSP
2017	CLN	A	21	0.99	2.00	2.87	1.9				
2017	MOD	A+	21	1.42	3.94	5.40	-0.1				
2018	JUP	A+	22	1.14	2.40	3.83	0.7				
2018	JAX	AA	22	1.24	3.79	4.42	1.2				
2019	JAX	AA	23	1.10	3.31	3.93	0.9				
2019	NWO	AAA	23	1.71	7.59	8.50	-0.9				
2019	MIA	MLB	23	1.46	5.77	6.38	-0.2	92.0	59.2	10.2	43.5
2020	MIA	MLB	24	1.45	5.25	5.39	0.4	91.8	60.9	10.5	44.8

Robert Dugger, continued

Pitch Shape vs LHH

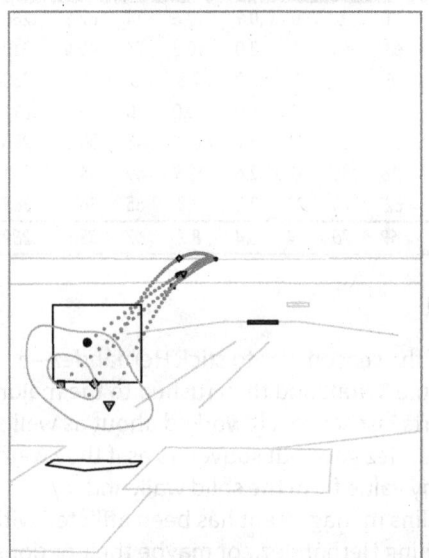

Pitch Shape vs RHH

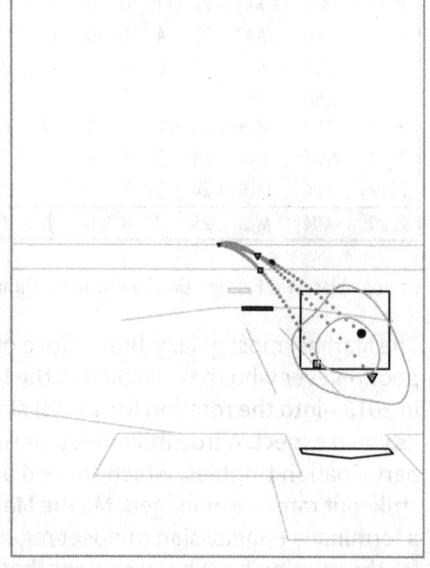

Type	Frequency	Velocity	H Movement	V Movement
● Fastball	35.2%	90.5 [94]	-7.7 [96]	-17.3 [96]
□ Sinker	23.9%	89.7 [85]	-13.9 [92]	-22.7 [92]
+ Cutter				
▲ Changeup	3.3%	79.3 [79]	-9.3 [109]	-30 [92]
✕ Splitter				
▽ Slider	24.5%	79.2 [78]	5.3 [101]	-39.6 [81]
◇ Curveball	13.0%	73 [81]	11.7 [117]	-52.7 [89]
⊕ Slow Curveball				
✱ Knuckleball				
▼ Screwball				

Miami Marlins 2020

Elieser Hernandez   RHP

Born: 05/03/95   Age: 25   Bats: R   Throws: R
Height: 6'0"   Weight: 210   Origin: International Free Agent, 2011

YEAR	TEAM	LVL	AGE	W	L	SV	G	GS	IP	H	HR	BB/9	K/9	K	GB%	BABIP
2017	AST	RK	22	1	0	0	3	2	10	6	0	0.9	12.6	14	62%	.286
2017	BCA	A+	22	4	5	0	15	11	63^1	55	6	3.0	10.5	74	40%	.310
2018	JUP	A+	23	0	1	0	2	2	6	9	2	6.0	7.5	5	68%	.350
2018	JAX	AA	23	0	0	0	2	2	9	7	3	4.0	10.0	10	23%	.211
2018	MIA	MLB	23	2	7	0	32	6	65^2	68	11	3.7	6.2	45	30%	.286
2019	NWO	AAA	24	3	1	0	9	9	48	35	0	2.6	12.9	69	34%	.315
2019	MIA	MLB	24	3	5	0	21	15	82^1	76	20	2.8	9.3	85	36%	.263
2020	MIA	MLB	25	3	4	0	45	6	69	70	14	3.4	8.7	67	33%	.289

Comparables: Wes Parsons, Dan Straily, Justin Dunn

The Marlins' most galaxy-brain move of the season was to stick Hernández—a poor reliever who they plucked in the Rule 5 draft and then rushed to the majors in 2018—into the rotation for 15 (!!!) starts last season. It worked about as well as you'd expect. A true millennial, Hernández gave out souvenirs as if they were participation trophies, which sapped any value from the solid walk and strikeout rates he managed. Maybe Marlins management has been afflicted with a terminally Panglossian mindset regarding Hernández...or maybe their options for the rotation have been so poor that Hernández actually did represent an improvement. But what's really the difference between self-inflicted lack of depth and a swift kick in the pants from the universe as far as pitching is concerned?

YEAR	TEAM	LVL	AGE	WHIP	ERA	DRA	WARP	MPH	FB%	WHF	CSP
2017	AST	RK	22	0.70	1.80	0.95	0.5				
2017	BCA	A+	22	1.20	3.98	4.33	0.6				
2018	JUP	A+	23	2.17	6.00	7.03	-0.1				
2018	JAX	AA	23	1.22	4.00	4.76	0.1				
2018	MIA	MLB	23	1.45	5.21	6.00	0.7	93.2	62.1	9.3	49.7
2019	NWO	AAA	24	1.02	1.12	1.45	2.4				
2019	MIA	MLB	24	1.24	5.03	4.78	0.9	93.1	55.3	12.1	48.9
2020	MIA	MLB	25	1.38	4.96	5.13	0.4	92.9	59.3	11.3	50.4

Elieser Hernandez, continued

Pitch Shape vs LHH

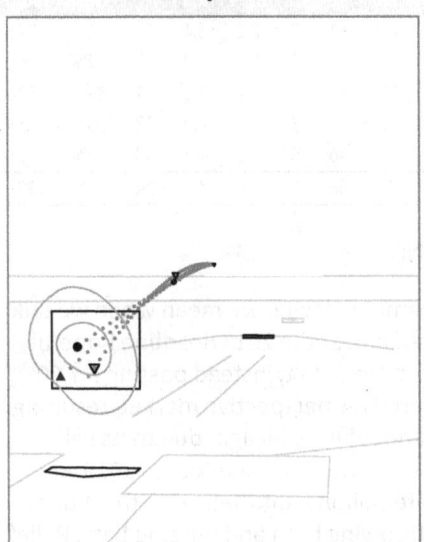

Pitch Shape vs RHH

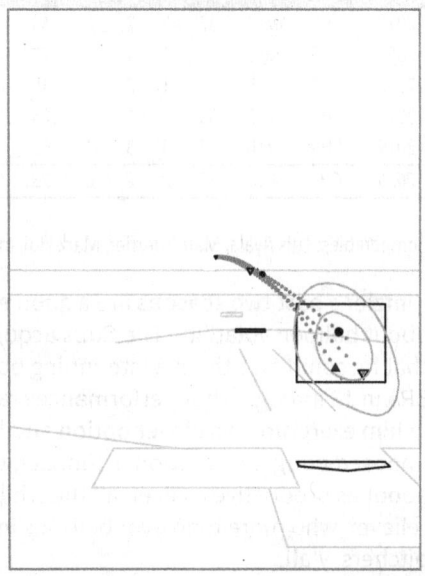

Type	Frequency	Velocity	H Movement	V Movement
● Fastball	53.9%	91 [96]	-6.1 [103]	-14.2 [104]
☐ Sinker				
+ Cutter				
▲ Changeup	11.3%	82.5 [90]	-12.6 [93]	-28.2 [98]
✕ Splitter				
▽ Slider	33.4%	78.7 [76]	9.5 [119]	-29 [112]
◇ Curveball				
◈ Slow Curveball				
✱ Knuckleball				
▼ Screwball				

Miami Marlins 2020

Brandon Kintzler   RHP
Born: 08/01/84   Age: 35   Bats: R   Throws: R
Height: 6'0"   Weight: 194   Origin: Round 40, 2004 Draft (#1182 overall)

YEAR	TEAM	LVL	AGE	W	L	SV	G	GS	IP	H	HR	BB/9	K/9	K	GB%	BABIP
2017	MIN	MLB	32	2	2	28	45	0	45^1	41	3	2.2	5.4	27	54%	.273
2017	WAS	MLB	32	2	1	1	27	0	26	25	2	1.7	4.2	12	57%	.267
2018	WAS	MLB	33	1	2	2	45	0	42^2	40	2	2.7	6.5	31	49%	.302
2018	CHN	MLB	33	2	1	0	25	0	18	27	3	4.5	6.0	12	53%	.381
2019	CHN	MLB	34	3	3	1	62	0	57	46	5	2.1	7.6	48	56%	.261
2020	CHN	MLB	35	2	2	0	33	0	35	38	5	2.4	6.7	26	54%	.307

Comparables: Luis Ayala, Matt Guerrier, Mark Huismann

Kintzler's past two seasons are a good example of what we mean when we talk about bullpen volatility. The Cubs acquired him at the 2018 deadline hopeful that he could give them a late-inning boost. He didn't, instead posting a 7.00 ERA in 18 innings. That performance cratered his perspective market, resulting in him exercising his player option and handcuffing Chicago (due to its self-imposed budget restrictions). Kintzler, then unwanted, went out in 2019 was about as productive as ever, all the while remaining antithetical to the modern reliever, who more than ever believes in throwing hard and missing bats. Relief pitchers, y'all.

YEAR	TEAM	LVL	AGE	WHIP	ERA	DRA	WARP	MPH	FB%	WHF	CSP
2017	MIN	MLB	32	1.15	2.78	4.76	0.2	95.2	80.9	6.5	46.9
2017	WAS	MLB	32	1.15	3.46	5.84	-0.2	95.1	83.2	4.8	54.7
2018	WAS	MLB	33	1.24	3.59	6.36	-0.7	94.4	83.6	7.4	48.9
2018	CHN	MLB	33	2.00	7.00	6.40	-0.3	94.6	85.8	8.4	45.4
2019	CHN	MLB	34	1.04	2.68	3.81	1.0	94.5	73.3	8.3	49.2
2020	CHN	MLB	35	1.37	4.64	4.75	0.3	93.4	78.1	7.3	47.9

Brandon Kintzler, continued

Pitch Shape vs LHH	Pitch Shape vs RHH
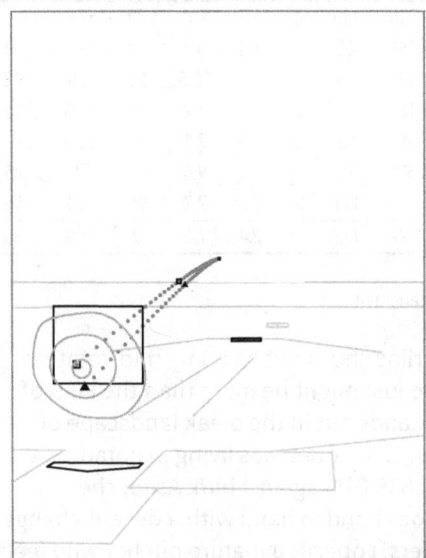	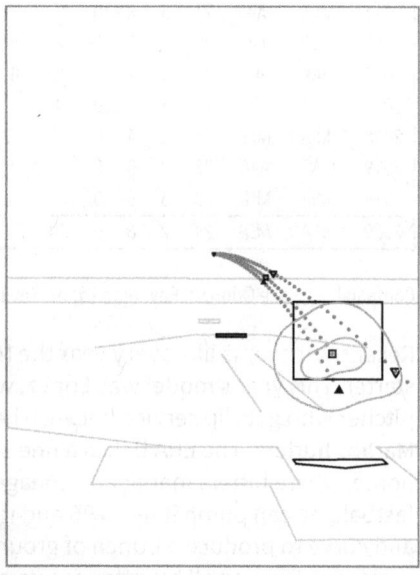

Type	Frequency	Velocity	H Movement	V Movement
● Fastball	3.6%	93.2 [102]	-9.4 [89]	-16.4 [99]
☐ Sinker	69.7%	92.9 [101]	-13.7 [93]	-20.4 [100]
+ Cutter				
▲ Changeup	16.6%	87.7 [109]	-14.5 [84]	-24.2 [109]
✕ Splitter				
▽ Slider	10.1%	87 [111]	-0.4 [78]	-29.2 [111]
◇ Curveball				
⊕ Slow Curveball				
✳ Knuckleball				
▼ Screwball				

Pablo López   RHP

Born: 03/07/96   Age: 24   Bats: L   Throws: R
Height: 6'3"   Weight: 200   Origin: International Free Agent, 2012

YEAR	TEAM	LVL	AGE	W	L	SV	G	GS	IP	H	HR	BB/9	K/9	K	GB%	BABIP
2017	MOD	A+	21	5	8	0	19	18	100	113	6	1.2	8.0	89	51%	.341
2017	JUP	A+	21	0	3	0	8	6	45^1	42	0	1.4	6.4	32	59%	.307
2018	JAX	AA	22	1	2	0	8	8	43^2	30	3	1.6	10.5	51	42%	.245
2018	NWO	AAA	22	1	1	0	4	4	18^2	16	3	1.9	7.2	15	47%	.236
2018	MIA	MLB	22	2	4	0	10	10	58^2	56	8	2.8	7.1	46	50%	.281
2019	NWO	AAA	23	0	0	0	2	2	9^1	10	0	2.9	9.6	10	62%	.385
2019	MIA	MLB	23	5	8	0	21	21	111^1	111	15	2.2	7.7	95	49%	.299
2020	MIA	MLB	24	7	8	0	24	24	129	123	17	2.4	7.5	107	48%	.285

Comparables: Jake Odorizzi, Reynaldo López, Kevin Gausman

Recently, it seems like every year the Marlins churn out a young, mid-rotation starter. This year's model was López, who just might be more than the kind of pitcher who gets lip service because he stands out in the bleak landscape of Marlins hurlers. The ERA belies a fine DRA, and López was living in paradise at home, where hitters managed a meager .638 OPS against him. As for the fastball, he can pump it up to 96 and it goes hand in hand with a decent change and curve to produce a bunch of grounders. López is a mature pitcher who feels comfortable using all his offerings versus both lefties and righties, even though he's a ripe 24 years old and was in High-A as recently as 2017. Although he missed two months in the middle of 2019 due to a right shoulder strain, López has the beat on a rotation spot for 2020 as the Marlins continue to take no action in the free agent market.

YEAR	TEAM	LVL	AGE	WHIP	ERA	DRA	WARP	MPH	FB%	WHF	CSP
2017	MOD	A+	21	1.26	5.04	4.68	0.6				
2017	JUP	A+	21	1.08	2.18	4.38	0.4				
2018	JAX	AA	22	0.87	0.62	2.58	1.4				
2018	NWO	AAA	22	1.07	3.38	3.18	0.5				
2018	MIA	MLB	22	1.26	4.14	4.58	0.5	95.1	60.4	11.7	46.5
2019	NWO	AAA	23	1.39	1.93	4.47	0.2				
2019	MIA	MLB	23	1.24	5.09	4.19	1.9	95.9	58.6	11.5	48.8
2020	MIA	MLB	24	1.22	3.71	4.03	2.6	95.5	60.9	11.9	49.2

Pablo López, continued

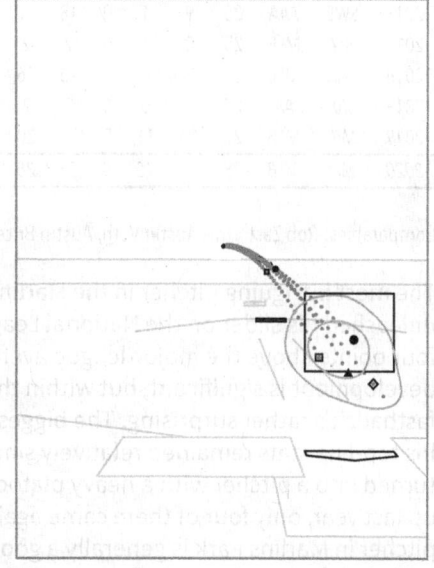

Type		Frequency	Velocity	H Movement	V Movement
●	Fastball	41.0%	94.1 [105]	-8.3 [94]	-16.9 [98]
□	Sinker	17.6%	93.7 [106]	-14.2 [90]	-22.6 [92]
+	Cutter				
▲	Changeup	22.0%	86.2 [103]	-15.1 [82]	-30.7 [90]
×	Splitter				
▽	Slider				
◇	Curveball	19.4%	80.2 [105]	10.1 [111]	-41 [114]
✦	Slow Curveball				
✱	Knuckleball				
▼	Screwball				

Caleb Smith   LHP

Born: 07/28/91   Age: 28   Bats: R   Throws: L
Height: 6'2"   Weight: 205   Origin: Round 14, 2013 Draft (#434 overall)

YEAR	TEAM	LVL	AGE	W	L	SV	G	GS	IP	H	HR	BB/9	K/9	K	GB%	BABIP
2017	SWB	AAA	25	9	1	0	18	17	98	75	7	2.6	8.9	97	42%	.264
2017	NYA	MLB	25	0	1	0	9	2	18²	21	4	4.8	8.7	18	28%	.315
2018	MIA	MLB	26	5	6	0	16	16	77¹	63	10	3.8	10.2	88	31%	.276
2019	JAX	AA	27	0	0	0	2	2	9¹	7	4	1.9	18.3	19	25%	.250
2019	MIA	MLB	27	10	11	0	28	28	153¹	128	33	3.5	9.9	168	28%	.251
2020	MIA	MLB	28	9	10	0	28	28	154	132	29	3.5	9.7	167	29%	.267

Comparables: Rob Zastryzny, Austin Voth, Austin Brice

The most intriguing pitcher in the Marlins rotation entering last season, Smith unleashed his slider on the National League and struck out 26 percent of hitters, four points above the major-league average for starters. That singular development is significant, but within the context of a real velocity drop on his fastball, it's rather surprising. The biggest impact from a results standpoint, as his top-line stats remained relatively similar to his 2018 season, was that Smith turned into a pitcher with a heavy platoon split. Out of the 33 homers he gave up last year, only four of them came against left-handed batters. A fly-ball pitcher in Marlins Park is generally a good thing though, even with the fences coming in, and Smith will once again be a key contributor in a still-developing Marlins rotation.

YEAR	TEAM	LVL	AGE	WHIP	ERA	DRA	WARP	MPH	FB%	WHF	CSP
2017	SWB	AAA	25	1.05	2.39	2.68	3.2				
2017	NYA	MLB	25	1.66	7.71	4.92	0.1	95.5	50.3	14.4	42.2
2018	MIA	MLB	26	1.24	4.19	4.05	1.1	94.8	59.1	13.3	48.7
2019	JAX	AA	27	0.96	5.79	2.83	0.2				
2019	MIA	MLB	27	1.23	4.52	4.55	2.0	93.9	53.7	13.8	47.3
2020	MIA	MLB	28	1.24	3.93	4.26	2.7	93.7	55.4	13.8	46.8

Caleb Smith, continued

Pitch Shape vs LHH

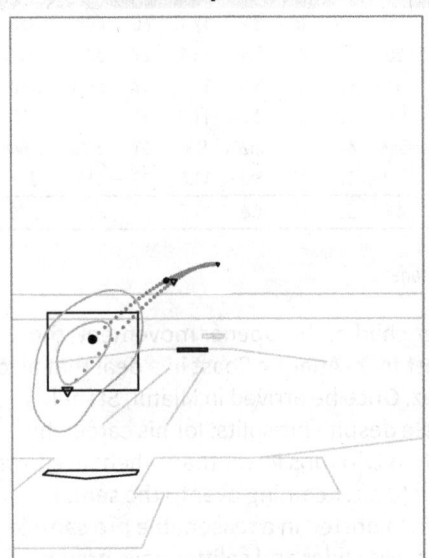

Pitch Shape vs RHH

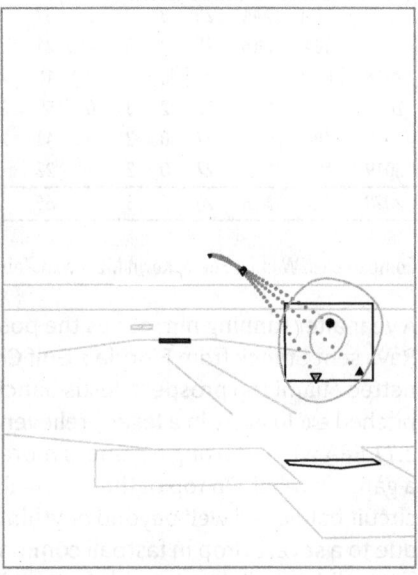

Type	Frequency	Velocity	H Movement	V Movement
● Fastball	53.7%	91.8 [98]	12.7 [74]	-14.9 [103]
☐ Sinker				
+ Cutter				
▲ Changeup	14.7%	82.9 [91]	14 [87]	-26.6 [102]
✕ Splitter				
▽ Slider	31.6%	83.8 [97]	-1.5 [85]	-31.7 [104]
◇ Curveball				
⊕ Slow Curveball				
✸ Knuckleball				
▼ Screwball				

Miami Marlins 2020

Ryne Stanek   RHP
Born: 07/26/91   Age: 28   Bats: R   Throws: R
Height: 6'4"   Weight: 225   Origin: Round 1, 2013 Draft (#29 overall)

YEAR	TEAM	LVL	AGE	W	L	SV	G	GS	IP	H	HR	BB/9	K/9	K	GB%	BABIP
2017	DUR	AAA	25	3	0	8	37	0	44^2	26	0	3.2	12.1	60	40%	.268
2017	TBA	MLB	25	0	0	0	21	0	20	26	6	5.4	13.1	29	33%	.417
2018	DUR	AAA	26	0	1	2	10	0	9^2	5	1	5.6	15.8	17	59%	.250
2018	TBA	MLB	26	2	3	0	59	29	66^1	45	8	3.7	11.0	81	32%	.253
2019	TBA	MLB	27	0	2	0	41	27	55^2	44	7	3.2	9.9	61	33%	.264
2019	MIA	MLB	27	0	2	1	22	0	21^1	17	4	8.0	11.8	28	31%	.271
2020	MIA	MLB	28	3	3	13	65	0	69	58	10	4.6	11.5	88	34%	.296

Comparables: Wander Suero, Kevin McGowan, Tobi Stoner

A year after running him out as the poster child of the Opener movement, the Rays sent Stanek from Florida's Gulf Coast to its Atlantic Coast in a deal that also netted Miami top prospect Jesús Sánchez. Once he arrived in Miami, Stanek pitched exclusively in a legacy reliever role despite his splits: for his career, his 2.71 ERA when starting a game is more than two runs lower than when he enters a game in relief. On top of that, his walk rate after coming over to the senior circuit ballooned well beyond anything he'd posted in a reasonable pro sample due to a severe drop in fastball command. His slider and splitter have grown into solid out pitches, and his fastball is still top-flight when he controls it. That enough will keep Stanek in the mix for high-leverage spots in 2020 and his fly-ball tendencies, while not ideal in this era, make for a good fit in Marlins Park.

YEAR	TEAM	LVL	AGE	WHIP	ERA	DRA	WARP	MPH	FB%	WHF	CSP
2017	DUR	AAA	25	0.94	1.21	2.33	1.5				
2017	TBA	MLB	25	1.90	5.85	2.67	0.6	100.3	67.1	16.3	44.4
2018	DUR	AAA	26	1.14	1.86	2.65	0.3				
2018	TBA	MLB	26	1.09	2.98	3.34	1.4	99.9	60.1	16.9	44.1
2019	TBA	MLB	27	1.15	3.40	4.92	0.4	99.5	57.4	16.7	42.4
2019	MIA	MLB	27	1.69	5.48	4.19	0.3	98.9	52	16.3	38.9
2020	MIA	MLB	28	1.35	3.89	4.12	1.0	99.0	58.8	16.8	43.3

Ryne Stanek, continued

Pitch Shape vs LHH	Pitch Shape vs RHH
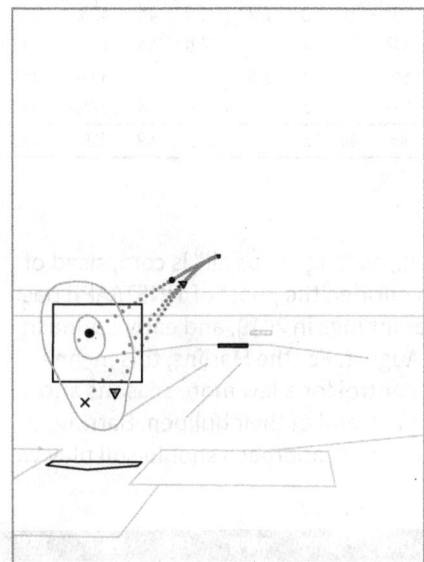	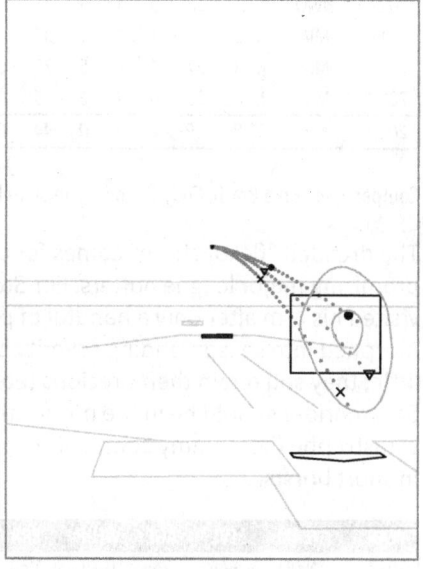

Type	Frequency	Velocity	H Movement	V Movement
● Fastball	55.7%	97.9 [116]	-7.7 [96]	-10.5 [114]
☐ Sinker				
+ Cutter				
▲ Changeup				
✕ Splitter	22.0%	88.4 [114]	-8.2 [99]	-27.3 [106]
▽ Slider	22.3%	90.1 [124]	0.4 [81]	-27.1 [117]
◇ Curveball				
⊕ Slow Curveball				
✱ Knuckleball				
▼ Screwball				

Drew Steckenrider   RHP

Born: 01/10/91   Age: 29   Bats: R   Throws: R
Height: 6'5"   Weight: 215   Origin: Round 8, 2012 Draft (#257 overall)

YEAR	TEAM	LVL	AGE	W	L	SV	G	GS	IP	H	HR	BB/9	K/9	K	GB%	BABIP
2017	NWO	AAA	26	0	1	5	26	0	33^1	18	3	2.2	11.9	44	43%	.217
2017	MIA	MLB	26	1	1	1	37	0	34^2	30	4	4.7	14.0	54	43%	.347
2018	MIA	MLB	27	4	4	5	71	0	64^2	55	7	3.8	10.3	74	34%	.296
2019	MIA	MLB	28	0	2	0	15	0	14^1	9	6	3.1	8.8	14	32%	.094
2020	MIA	MLB	29	2	2	0	44	0	46	44	8	3.6	9.6	49	35%	.292

Comparables: Brad Brach, Cody Carroll, Ryne Stanek

The dreaded "flexor strain" comes for us all, as long as "us all" is comprised of promising major league hurlers. For Steckenrider, the ghost of TINSTAAPP past visited his arm after only a handful of poor innings in 2019, and early optimism morphed into season-ending severity by August. For the Marlins, this means little; they still retain their precious team control for a few more seasons and Steckenrider should be in the mix for the back end of their bullpen. Barring catastrophe (i.e. Tommy John), his fastball-heavy approach should still play well in short bursts.

YEAR	TEAM	LVL	AGE	WHIP	ERA	DRA	WARP	MPH	FB%	WHF	CSP
2017	NWO	AAA	26	0.78	1.62	1.26	1.5				
2017	MIA	MLB	26	1.38	2.34	3.70	0.6	97.3	77.8	14.8	49.9
2018	MIA	MLB	27	1.27	3.90	4.44	0.4	96.8	76.4	12.2	50.8
2019	MIA	MLB	28	0.98	6.28	5.93	-0.1	96.4	62	9.3	48.3
2020	MIA	MLB	29	1.35	4.50	4.75	0.3	96.2	74.6	12.5	49.5

Drew Steckenrider, continued

Pitch Shape vs LHH	Pitch Shape vs RHH
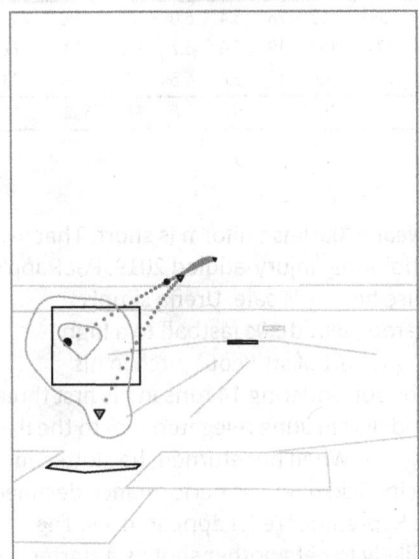	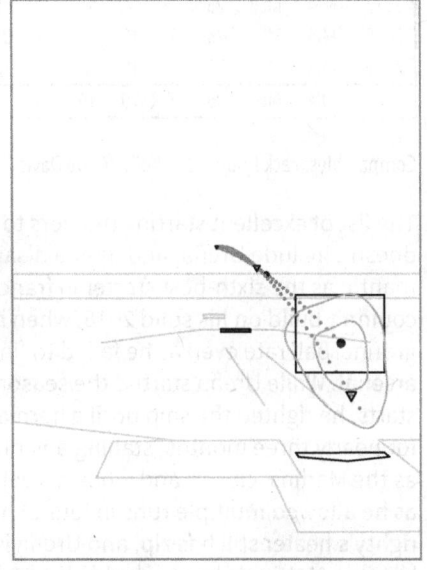

Type	Frequency	Velocity	H Movement	V Movement
● Fastball	62.0%	95.1 [108]	-8 [95]	-10.6 [114]
☐ Sinker				
+ Cutter				
▲ Changeup				
✕ Splitter				
▽ Slider	38.0%	83 [94]	1.8 [86]	-39.8 [81]
◇ Curveball				
⊕ Slow Curveball				
✱ Knuckleball				
▼ Screwball				

Miami Marlins 2020

José Ureña RHP
Born: 09/12/91   Age: 28   Bats: R   Throws: R
Height: 6'2"   Weight: 200   Origin: International Free Agent, 2008

YEAR	TEAM	LVL	AGE	W	L	SV	G	GS	IP	H	HR	BB/9	K/9	K	GB%	BABIP
2017	MIA	MLB	25	14	7	0	34	28	169²	152	26	3.4	6.0	113	44%	.249
2018	MIA	MLB	26	9	12	0	31	31	174	155	19	2.6	6.7	130	51%	.272
2019	MIA	MLB	27	4	10	3	24	13	84²	99	13	2.8	6.6	62	50%	.323
2020	MIA	MLB	28	7	10	10	58	19	141	157	20	3.0	7.0	111	50%	.314

Comparables: Zack Britton, Joe Kelly, Wade Davis

The list of excellent starting pitchers to wear a Marlins uniform is short. That list doesn't include Ureña, and after a disappointing, injury-addled 2019, Pat Rapp's mantle as the sixth-best starter in franchise history is safe. Ureña simply couldn't build on his solid 2018, when he rode a mid-90s fastball to a high ground-ball rate even as he failed to find any sort of strikeout pitch in his arsenal. While Ureña started the season by surrendering 14 runs in his first three starts, he righted the ship until a herniated disc in June relegated him to the IL for nearly three months, stalling any progress. When he returned, he slotted in as the Marlins' closer; and while his velocity ticked up, his performance declined as he allowed multiple runs in four of his September relief appearances. The righty's heater still has zip, and Ureña is likely to get another shot as a starter, but Don Mattingly has to decide if a 16 percent career strikeout rate belongs in even Miami's rotation. At some point, a pitching development machine needs to churn out one or two stars. The Marlins appear to have bought an aftermarket Joe Kelly mold.

YEAR	TEAM	LVL	AGE	WHIP	ERA	DRA	WARP	MPH	FB%	WHF	CSP
2017	MIA	MLB	25	1.27	3.82	5.25	0.5	97.6	56.2	9.1	45.2
2018	MIA	MLB	26	1.18	3.98	4.01	2.6	97.9	58.8	9.7	46.2
2019	MIA	MLB	27	1.48	5.21	5.73	0.0	97.9	63.1	10.4	44.8
2020	MIA	MLB	28	1.45	4.89	4.99	1.1	97.2	59.4	9.7	45.6

José Ureña, continued

Pitch Shape vs LHH	Pitch Shape vs RHH
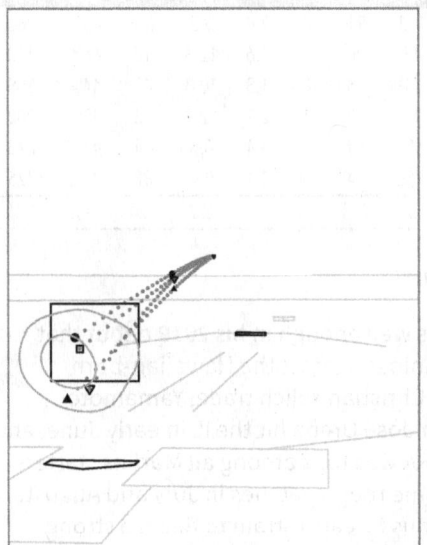	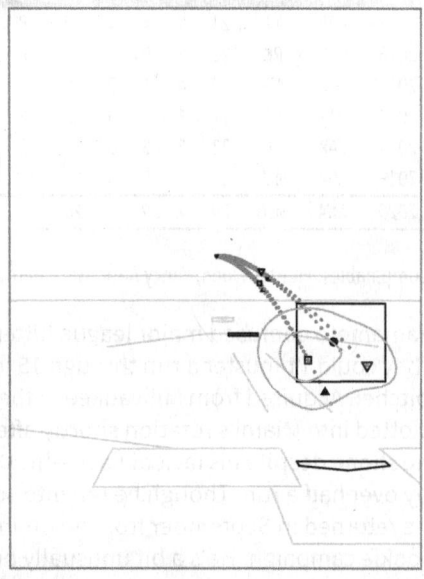

Type	Frequency	Velocity	H Movement	V Movement
● Fastball	7.2%	95.2 [108]	-12.3 [76]	-17.1 [97]
☐ Sinker	55.8%	96.4 [120]	-14.3 [90]	-18.5 [106]
+ Cutter				
▲ Changeup	10.7%	90.6 [119]	-13.7 [88]	-22.6 [114]
✕ Splitter				
▽ Slider	26.3%	85.9 [107]	2.8 [91]	-28.4 [114]
◇ Curveball				
✦ Slow Curveball				
✱ Knuckleball				
▼ Screwball				

Jordan Yamamoto RHP

Born: 05/11/96 Age: 24 Bats: R Throws: R
Height: 6'0" Weight: 185 Origin: Round 12, 2014 Draft (#356 overall)

YEAR	TEAM	LVL	AGE	W	L	SV	G	GS	IP	H	HR	BB/9	K/9	K	GB%	BABIP
2017	CAR	A+	21	9	4	1	22	18	111	91	8	2.4	9.2	113	40%	.286
2018	MRL	RK	22	1	0	0	3	3	11	5	1	1.6	12.3	15	64%	.190
2018	JUP	A+	22	4	1	0	7	7	40^2	26	0	1.8	10.4	47	44%	.268
2018	JAX	AA	22	1	0	0	3	3	17	12	1	2.1	12.2	23	45%	.282
2019	JAX	AA	23	3	5	0	12	12	65^1	53	7	3.4	8.8	64	47%	.275
2019	MIA	MLB	23	4	5	0	15	15	78^2	54	11	4.1	9.4	82	37%	.225
2020	MIA	MLB	24	7	9	0	26	26	135	123	20	3.7	8.3	124	39%	.276

Comparables: Hunter Wood, Yency Almonte, Pablo López

Yamamoto confused major league hitters well enough in his 2019 debut that they couldn't muster a run through 15 innings against the Hawaiian-born pitcher. Acquired from Milwaukee in the Christian Yelich trade, Yamamoto slotted into Miami's rotation shortly after José Ureña hit the IL in early June, and he shone despite his lack of flash—his DRA was tops among all Marlins starters by over half a run. Though he ran into some rough patches in July and August, he returned in September from an ominous forearm strain to finish a strong rookie campaign. He's a bit unusually built for a pitcher, with short legs and a long torso, and the margin for error with his control is slim, but Yamamoto's strong slider and workmanlike fastball may have already punched his ticket to fourth starterdom.

YEAR	TEAM	LVL	AGE	WHIP	ERA	DRA	WARP	MPH	FB%	WHF	CSP
2017	CAR	A+	21	1.09	2.51	3.36	2.4				
2018	MRL	RK	22	0.64	2.45	0.90	0.6				
2018	JUP	A+	22	0.84	1.55	2.46	1.4				
2018	JAX	AA	22	0.94	2.12	2.99	0.5				
2019	JAX	AA	23	1.19	3.58	4.53	0.3				
2019	MIA	MLB	23	1.14	4.46	3.56	1.9	93.8	50.2	10.1	46.9
2020	MIA	MLB	24	1.32	4.10	4.36	2.2	93.6	51.7	10.5	48.3

Jordan Yamamoto, continued

Pitch Shape vs LHH

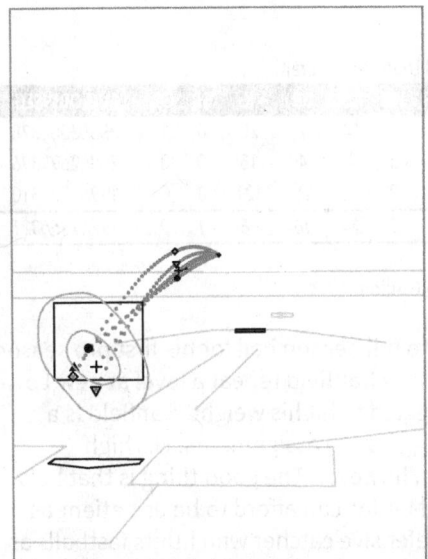

Pitch Shape vs RHH

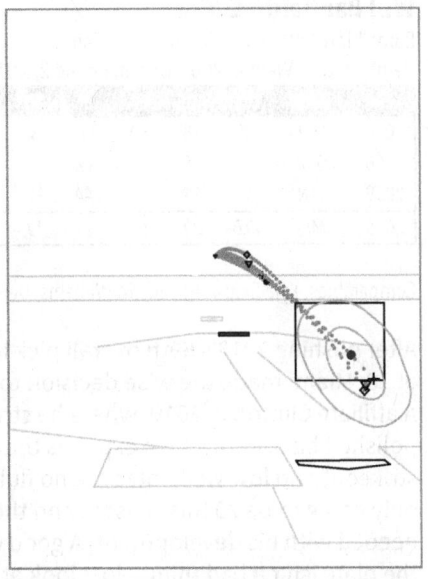

Type	Frequency	Velocity	H Movement	V Movement
● Fastball	48.0%	91.9 [98]	-5.8 [105]	-13.5 [106]
☐ Sinker				
+ Cutter	17.7%	86.2 [84]	3.1 [107]	-28.8 [82]
▲ Changeup	3.1%	82.7 [91]	-13.2 [91]	-30.1 [92]
✕ Splitter				
▽ Slider	15.1%	79.4 [79]	13 [134]	-43.9 [69]
◇ Curveball	13.9%	74.7 [87]	10.6 [113]	-57.1 [80]
◈ Slow Curveball				
✻ Knuckleball				
▼ Screwball				

PLAYER COMMENTS WITHOUT GRAPHS

Will Banfield   C
Born: 11/18/99   Age: 20   Bats: R   Throws: R
Height: 6'0"   Weight: 200   Origin: Round 2, 2018 Draft (#69 overall)

YEAR	TEAM	LVL	AGE	PA	R	2B	3B	HR	RBI	BB	K	SB	CS	AVG/OBP/SLG
2018	MRL	RK	18	94	7	8	1	0	14	7	28	0	1	.256/.330/.378
2018	GRB	A	18	52	5	0	0	3	4	4	15	0	0	.208/.269/.396
2019	CLN	A	19	433	44	13	2	9	55	25	121	0	0	.199/.252/.310
2020	MIA	MLB	20	251	21	11	1	5	24	16	88	1	0	.197/.256/.321

Comparables: Kyle Skipworth, Justin Williams, Deivy Grullon

After pushing 2018's 69th overall pick into full-season ball for his first pro season at 18, Miami made the wise decision to have Banfield repeat a level at new Low-A affiliate Clinton in 2019, where he struggled to hit his weight. Banfield is a polished backstop, which explains the aggressive assignments. His high strikeout and low walk rates are no fluke, however. The good thing is that he's only going to be 20 this season, and the Marlins can afford to be as patient as needed with his development. A good defensive catcher who hunts fastballs at the plate isn't a bad thing—just look at Banfield's senior, Jorge Alfaro—but developing Banfield's hit tool into something...nicer...will be his and Miami's priority as he ascends in the system.

YEAR	TEAM	LVL	AGE	PA	DRC+	VORP	BABIP	BRR	FRAA	WARP
2018	MRL	RK	18	94	82	1.8	.375	-0.9	C(22): 1.2	0.3
2018	GRB	A	18	52	76	0.7	.233	0.1	C(14): 0.1	0.1
2019	CLN	A	19	433	53	-1.4	.256	-1.7	C(91): 5.5	0.2
2020	MIA	MLB	20	251	53	-7.8	.291	-0.3	C 0	-0.8

JJ Bleday OF

Born: 11/10/97 Age: 22 Bats: L Throws: L
Height: 6'3" Weight: 205 Origin: Round 1, 2019 Draft (#4 overall)

YEAR	TEAM	LVL	AGE	PA	R	2B	3B	HR	RBI	BB	K	SB	CS	AVG/OBP/SLG
2019	JUP	A+	21	151	13	8	0	3	19	11	29	0	0	.257/.311/.379
2020	MIA	MLB	22	251	23	12	1	6	25	16	66	2	1	.224/.277/.355

Comparables: Yangervis Solarte, Rymer Liriano, Abraham Almonte

The top-of-the-first-round college outfielder is a relatively rare specimen these days, but Bleday sports the sort of mature approach that compels a team to snag such a player that early. He can adjust mid-swing to get the barrel to the ball even when beaten, and he has good power, evidenced by his Division-I leading home run total in 2019. While already a corner outfielder, which may give some pause, he has a strong arm and average speed/acceleration on the grass that should allow him to stick in right field for a while. Miami assigned him somewhat aggressively to High-A Jupiter, and his profile—lefty power hitter with an advanced approach—gives the organization the type of player they've been starved for, as they stockpile role-55 arms and toolsy infielders. Marrying his bat-to-ball skills with his penchant for power is key to Bleday's success, and he'll get to work on that union in his first full season of pro ball in 2020.

YEAR	TEAM	LVL	AGE	PA	DRC+	VORP	BABIP	BRR	FRAA	WARP
2019	JUP	A+	21	151	105	2.1	.306	-1.1	RF(32): -0.9	0.1
2020	MIA	MLB	22	251	68	-2.3	.287	0.0	RF -5	-0.7

Miami Marlins 2020

Jazz Chisholm SS

Born: 02/01/98 Age: 22 Bats: L Throws: R
Height: 5'11" Weight: 165 Origin: International Free Agent, 2015

YEAR	TEAM	LVL	AGE	PA	R	2B	3B	HR	RBI	BB	K	SB	CS	AVG/OBP/SLG
2017	KNC	A	19	125	14	5	2	1	12	10	39	3	0	.248/.325/.358
2018	KNC	A	20	341	52	17	4	15	43	30	97	8	2	.244/.311/.472
2018	VIS	A+	20	160	27	6	2	10	27	9	52	9	2	.329/.369/.597
2019	WTN	AA	21	364	51	6	5	18	44	41	123	13	4	.204/.305/.427
2019	JAX	AA	21	94	6	4	2	3	10	11	24	3	0	.284/.383/.494
2020	MIA	MLB	22	35	3	1	0	1	4	3	13	1	0	.205/.278/.366

Comparables: Yu Chang, Michael Chavis, Trevor Story

Double-A can be a reckoning for players like Chisholm. The plus-everything in the field remains plus, but the bat—with its surprising pop but high potential for swing-and-miss—faces perhaps its first real challenge. For Chisholm, the reckoning came while still in Arizona's system, when he barely managed to crack a .200 batting average and .300 OBP in Jackson. It may appear that the titillating Chisholm-for-Zac Gallen swap at the trade deadline energized the Bahamian shortstop, but in reality, Chisholm was making adjustments in the weeks prior to the trade, and manifested in a nice stat line when he added the "ville" to his chest. Most importantly, he cut his 34 percent strikeout rate down to a manageable 25 percent; for a player who exhibits a rather violent approach, gaining that much contact has outsized benefit.

YEAR	TEAM	LVL	AGE	PA	DRC+	VORP	BABIP	BRR	FRAA	WARP
2017	KNC	A	19	125	92	6.4	.371	0.7	SS(29): 0.8	0.6
2018	KNC	A	20	341	102	17.7	.303	-1.4	SS(75): -0.3	1.3
2018	VIS	A+	20	160	139	21.1	.443	0.5	SS(36): -0.7	1.3
2019	WTN	AA	21	364	108	19.9	.261	2.9	SS(88): -5.8	1.7
2019	JAX	AA	21	94	104	10.2	.370	-0.5	SS(21): -1.8	0.4
2020	MIA	MLB	22	35	70	-0.1	.311	0.0	SS 0	0.0

Monte Harrison OF

Born: 08/10/95 Age: 24 Bats: R Throws: R
Height: 6'3" Weight: 220 Origin: Round 2, 2014 Draft (#50 overall)

YEAR	TEAM	LVL	AGE	PA	R	2B	3B	HR	RBI	BB	K	SB	CS	AVG/OBP/SLG
2017	WIS	A	21	261	32	12	1	11	32	29	70	11	3	.265/.359/.475
2017	CAR	A+	21	252	41	16	1	10	35	14	69	16	1	.278/.341/.487
2018	JAX	AA	22	583	85	20	3	19	48	44	215	28	9	.240/.316/.399
2019	NWO	AAA	23	244	41	7	2	9	24	25	73	20	2	.274/.357/.451
2020	MIA	MLB	24	112	10	5	1	2	11	8	41	3	1	.215/.288/.343

Comparables: Lane Thomas, Brett Phillips, Teoscar Hernández

Harrison owns one of 2019's most bizarre seasons for any top prospect. His obscene number of strikeouts in Double-A in 2018 were enough to tarnish his prospect shine, but he came out mashing in New Orleans last year with a strikeout rate below 30 percent and was selected to play in the Futures Game. He then injured his wrist in late June diving for a ball, tried to stay in the game and ultimately was pulled after setting up in the lefty batter's box, even though, like Inigo Montoyo, he's not left-handed. Harrison subsequently hit the IL, missed the Futures Game and got surgery on his wrist, missing most of the rest of the season. Whereas he had previously been ticketed for a September call-up and competition for an outfield spot this spring, he's now a 24-year-old coming off a significant injury needing to hold gains made by retooling his swing.

YEAR	TEAM	LVL	AGE	PA	DRC+	VORP	BABIP	BRR	FRAA	WARP
2017	WIS	A	21	261	132	22.1	.333	1.3	CF(62): 1.6	2.1
2017	CAR	A+	21	252	127	20.5	.358	3.3	CF(32): -1.8, RF(24): 2.1	1.8
2018	JAX	AA	22	583	96	28.5	.368	3.6	CF(121): -8.0, RF(14): 0.4	1.3
2019	NWO	AAA	23	244	94	12.5	.373	3.2	CF(32): 2.6, RF(19): -2.4	0.9
2020	MIA	MLB	24	112	67	-0.9	.332	0.3	CF 0, RF 0	-0.1

Víctor Víctor Mesa OF

Born: 07/20/96   Age: 23   Bats: R   Throws: R
Height: 5'10"   Weight: 165   Origin: International Free Agent, 2018

YEAR	TEAM	LVL	AGE	PA	R	2B	3B	HR	RBI	BB	K	SB	CS	AVG/OBP/SLG
2019	JUP	A+	22	390	37	5	3	0	26	19	48	15	2	.252/.295/.283
2019	JAX	AA	22	113	8	2	0	0	3	3	16	3	0	.178/.200/.196
2020	MIA	MLB	23	35	3	1	0	0	3	2	7	1	0	.227/.268/.300

Comparables: Rafael Bautista, Engelb Vielma, David Fletcher

The man often compared to Albert Almora has begun to hit like Albert Almora … except Mesa did it in Double-A during 2019, which does not bode well for the highly touted international signee. It was Mesa's first time back in game action after an extended layoff, which could be a blessing (he just needs to shake the rust) or a curse (he lost vital development time and likely won't recover). The elements that made him an attractive prospect remain, since he can still run very well and play a good center field with a strong arm, but Mesa's penchant for contact at the plate won't be much of an asset if it continues to result in less pop than a Whole Foods.

YEAR	TEAM	LVL	AGE	PA	DRC+	VORP	BABIP	BRR	FRAA	WARP
2019	JUP	A+	22	390	90	1.2	.287	-0.9	CF(75): -3.3	0.3
2019	JAX	AA	22	113	16	-6.9	.209	-0.4	CF(25): 6.0	0.1
2020	MIA	MLB	23	35	49	-1.0	.275	0.0	CF 0	-0.1

Kameron Misner CF

Born: 01/08/98   Age: 22   Bats: L   Throws: L
Height: 6'4"   Weight: 219   Origin: Round 1, 2019 Draft (#35 overall)

YEAR	TEAM	LVL	AGE	PA	R	2B	3B	HR	RBI	BB	K	SB	CS	AVG/OBP/SLG
2019	MRL	RK	21	38	2	2	0	0	4	9	7	3	0	.241/.421/.310
2019	CLN	A	21	158	25	7	0	2	20	21	35	8	0	.276/.380/.373
2020	MIA	MLB	22	251	24	12	1	5	24	24	73	3	1	.225/.304/.345

Comparables: Darrell Ceciliani, Mitch Haniger, Jacob May

Friends call me Kam Misner / Whatever I touch / Clears the fence in the clutch / I'm too much! Misner is a big boy with big power and big speed. He lofts the ball with the best of 'em, and he can play across the outfield or at first base. Misner's patience allows him to wait for pitches to drive, which he did with regularity at Mizzou, even if that power didn't show up during his abbreviated pro debut in 2019. More professional reps will give Misner the opportunity to display whether he is content to be a Three True Outcomes guy with ridiculous power or if he'll temper his approach in order to max out the hit tool. Regardless of his future shape of production, he's a remarkably attractive prospect with both a high floor and a high ceiling.

YEAR	TEAM	LVL	AGE	PA	DRC+	VORP	BABIP	BRR	FRAA	WARP
2019	MRL	RK	21	38	139	3.7	.318	0.4	CF(5): -0.1, RF(3): -0.2	0.2
2019	CLN	A	21	158	137	11.1	.357	2.2	CF(30): 7.1	2.0
2020	MIA	MLB	22	251	76	0.3	.311	0.0	CF 7, RF 0	0.8

Miami Marlins 2020

Connor Scott OF
Born: 10/08/99 Age: 20 Bats: L Throws: L
Height: 6'4" Weight: 180 Origin: Round 1, 2018 Draft (#13 overall)

YEAR	TEAM	LVL	AGE	PA	R	2B	3B	HR	RBI	BB	K	SB	CS	AVG/OBP/SLG
2018	MRL	RK	18	119	15	1	4	0	8	14	29	8	5	.223/.319/.311
2018	GRB	A	18	89	4	2	0	1	5	10	27	1	3	.211/.295/.276
2019	CLN	A	19	413	56	24	4	4	36	31	91	21	9	.251/.311/.368
2019	JUP	A+	19	111	12	4	1	1	5	11	26	2	1	.235/.306/.327
2020	MIA	MLB	20	251	21	11	1	3	21	20	73	4	3	.213/.280/.316

Comparables: Carlos Tocci, Anthony Gose, Joe Benson

You would prefer your high school position player draftees carry a higher ceiling than Scott, but the Marlins' 2018 first-rounder hit adequately enough for a teenager after an aggressive promotion to High-A in July; his acceleration parrying the doubters for at least one more season. Miami seems to have guys like Scott by the bushel, propped up by good outfield defense and athleticism, but many of them are older and at a more advanced level than he is. A 20-year-old ticketed for a return engagement in the Florida State League in 2020, he will need to rein in his sometimes hitchy, looped swing as he ascends through the minors.

YEAR	TEAM	LVL	AGE	PA	DRC+	VORP	BABIP	BRR	FRAA	WARP
2018	MRL	RK	18	119	90	0.5	.307	-1.2	CF(22): -1.6	0.0
2018	GRB	A	18	89	56	-2.5	.300	-1.9	CF(22): -3.0	-0.7
2019	CLN	A	19	413	98	12.6	.322	1.6	CF(85): -2.6, LF(1): -0.1	1.1
2019	JUP	A+	19	111	85	3.0	.301	0.9	CF(24): -1.5	0.1
2020	MIA	MLB	20	251	61	-4.9	.298	-0.2	CF -2, LF 0	-0.7

Jesús Sánchez OF

Born: 10/07/97   Age: 22   Bats: L   Throws: R
Height: 6'3"   Weight: 230   Origin: International Free Agent, 2014

YEAR	TEAM	LVL	AGE	PA	R	2B	3B	HR	RBI	BB	K	SB	CS	AVG/OBP/SLG
2017	BGR	A	19	512	81	29	4	15	82	32	91	7	2	.305/.348/.478
2018	PCH	A+	20	378	56	24	2	10	64	15	71	6	3	.301/.331/.462
2018	MNT	AA	20	110	14	8	0	1	11	11	21	1	1	.214/.300/.327
2019	MNT	AA	21	316	32	11	1	8	49	24	65	5	4	.275/.332/.404
2019	NWO	AAA	21	78	11	1	0	4	9	9	15	0	0	.246/.338/.446
2019	DUR	AAA	21	71	6	2	1	1	5	6	20	0	0	.206/.282/.317
2020	MIA	MLB	22	42	4	2	0	1	4	3	11	0	0	.239/.289/.379

Comparables: Jorge Bonifacio, Justin Williams, Gabriel Guerrero

Carrying his very consistent offensive profile from the Rays to the Marlins in the Nick Anderson trade, Sánchez hasn't really taken that next big step since tearing up the Midwest League in 2017 as a teenager. The big outfielder doesn't hurt you in the field or on the bases, but neither of those skills are the crux of his future value. That lies in his lumber, and most specifically his power. Only problem is that it hasn't shown up in games yet to the extent that is expected—the Dominican native has not eclipsed 15 homers in any of his full pro seasons. The bat-to-ball skills remain solid, but even exceptional barrel control and a top-50 prospect pedigree can't stave off worries that Sánchez has set up camp on a performance plateau as a 22-year-old knocking on the door to the majors.

YEAR	TEAM	LVL	AGE	PA	DRC+	VORP	BABIP	BRR	FRAA	WARP
2017	BGR	A	19	512	127	29.7	.349	3.4	LF(78): 14.0, RF(19): -0.5	4.3
2018	PCH	A+	20	378	137	19.9	.350	-1.5	RF(78): 1.8, CF(7): -1.4	2.0
2018	MNT	AA	20	110	92	-0.8	.263	0.7	RF(26): -0.8, CF(1): 0.0	0.1
2019	MNT	AA	21	316	122	10.2	.327	0.1	RF(72): 0.0	1.4
2019	NWO	AAA	21	78	74	-2.5	.250	0.3	CF(8): -1.6, RF(7): 3.6	0.2
2019	DUR	AAA	21	71	52	-6.2	.279	-0.3	RF(15): 0.7	-0.2
2020	MIA	MLB	22	42	78	-0.3	.308	-0.1	RF 0	0.0

Edward Cabrera RHP

Born: 04/13/98 Age: 22 Bats: R Throws: R
Height: 6'4" Weight: 175 Origin: International Free Agent, 2015

YEAR	TEAM	LVL	AGE	W	L	SV	G	GS	IP	H	HR	BB/9	K/9	K	GB%	BABIP
2017	BAT	A-	19	1	3	0	13	6	35^2	42	1	2.0	8.1	32	55%	.350
2018	GRB	A	20	4	8	0	22	22	100^1	105	11	3.8	8.3	93	44%	.329
2019	JUP	A+	21	5	3	0	11	11	58	37	1	2.8	11.3	73	49%	.277
2019	JAX	AA	21	4	1	0	8	8	38^2	28	6	3.0	10.0	43	50%	.242
2020	MIA	MLB	22	2	2	0	29	2	37	37	6	3.9	9.3	38	44%	.313

Comparables: Jake Faria, Yordano Ventura, Gerrit Cole

Tall, slight and nasty. Young, projectable and breaking out before our eyes. Cabrera ripped through his initial Florida State League assignment en route to Jacksonville, where he was more than three years younger than league average and continued to strike out hitters with his mid- to upper-90s fastball and whiff-inducing slider. Making the leap to Double A as a 21-year-old pitcher is a significant step, and Cabrera made marked improvements by flashing an average changeup and suppressing the walks that clouded his 2018 performance. Concerns about the long-term viability of his changeup and a violent delivery are salient, and he's still a riskier prospect because of those concerns, but Cabrera showed he has at least mid-rotation potential. The 2020 season will not only be important in terms of in-game development, but in workload; even by today's standards, a true starter needs to be able to throw more than 100 innings per season.

YEAR	TEAM	LVL	AGE	WHIP	ERA	DRA	WARP	MPH	FB%	WHF	CSP
2017	BAT	A-	19	1.40	5.30	6.17	-0.4				
2018	GRB	A	20	1.47	4.22	5.33	-0.2				
2019	JUP	A+	21	0.95	2.02	3.04	1.4				
2019	JAX	AA	21	1.06	2.56	3.43	0.7				
2020	MIA	MLB	22	1.45	4.81	4.95	0.2				

Braxton Garrett   LHP

Born: 08/05/97   Age: 22   Bats: L   Throws: L
Height: 6'3"   Weight: 190   Origin: Round 1, 2016 Draft (#7 overall)

YEAR	TEAM	LVL	AGE	W	L	SV	G	GS	IP	H	HR	BB/9	K/9	K	GB%	BABIP
2017	GRB	A	19	1	0	0	4	4	15^1	13	3	3.5	9.4	16	49%	.250
2019	JUP	A+	21	6	6	0	20	20	105	92	13	3.2	10.1	118	54%	.294
2020	MIA	MLB	22	2	2	0	33	0	35	36	6	4.1	8.5	33	42%	.300

Comparables: Sal Romano, Kyle Ryan, Victor Arano

He's finally healthy! Garrett not only returned from Tommy John surgery in 2019 after almost two full years away from game action—he tossed over 100 innings, no small feat for the former first-rounder. The fastball-curveball combo that was fawned over in his amateur days mowed down High-A hitters, and he kept the ball down showing his mettle as a ground-ball pitcher. Asking any pitcher, even one as talented as Garrett, to work on regaining some fastball velocity and command in the wake of his extended absence while making the leap to the high minors is a tall order. A strong showing in the first half of the year would accelerate his timeline to Miami, but simply staying on the mound for the full season would be a win for the organization that has seen every Braxton in major-league history pass through its dimly-lit corridors.

YEAR	TEAM	LVL	AGE	WHIP	ERA	DRA	WARP	MPH	FB%	WHF	CSP
2017	GRB	A	19	1.24	2.93	4.86	0.1				
2019	JUP	A+	21	1.23	3.34	4.85	0.2				
2020	MIA	MLB	22	1.48	4.97	5.15	0.1				

Miami Marlins 2020

Jorge Guzman RHP

Born: 01/28/96 Age: 24 Bats: R Throws: R
Height: 6'2" Weight: 182 Origin: International Free Agent, 2014

YEAR	TEAM	LVL	AGE	W	L	SV	G	GS	IP	H	HR	BB/9	K/9	K	GB%	BABIP
2017	STA	A-	21	5	3	0	13	13	66^2	51	4	2.4	11.9	88	55%	.311
2018	JUP	A+	22	0	9	0	21	21	96	84	7	6.0	9.5	101	40%	.303
2019	JAX	AA	23	7	11	0	25	24	138^2	96	13	4.6	8.2	127	34%	.241
2020	MIA	MLB	24	2	2	0	33	0	35	36	5	3.9	7.8	30	35%	.298

Comparables: Matt Hall, Hansel Robles, André Rienzo

Maybe it was the weight of expectations sitting on him that led to Guzmán's disappointing 2018 season. "We got him for Stanton and he does this???," they cried. Those burdens seemed to have lifted for 2019; the young righty can still touch triple digits, and he improved his change and slider while getting stretched out at Double A last season. For Guzmán, though, enough concerns remain that he won't be making any global top prospect lists again soon. The free passes that doomed his 2018 campaign didn't entirely disappear, as he still posted a walk rate north of 12 percent. No matter how good the raw stuff is, the path to a major-league starting role is through the strike zone. As it is, the fireballer looks destined to be a three-pitch, late-inning reliever—a good outcome for a pitching prospect, but not what you want from the non-monetary headliner of the trade that sent the best power hitter in franchise history packing.

YEAR	TEAM	LVL	AGE	WHIP	ERA	DRA	WARP	MPH	FB%	WHF	CSP
2017	STA	A-	21	1.03	2.30	3.42	1.4				
2018	JUP	A+	22	1.54	4.03	5.77	-0.5				
2019	JAX	AA	23	1.20	3.50	4.16	1.3				
2020	MIA	MLB	24	1.46	4.77	4.95	0.2				

Nick Neidert   RHP

Born: 11/20/96   Age: 23   Bats: R   Throws: R
Height: 6'1"   Weight: 202   Origin: Round 2, 2015 Draft (#60 overall)

YEAR	TEAM	LVL	AGE	W	L	SV	G	GS	IP	H	HR	BB/9	K/9	K	GB%	BABIP
2017	MOD	A+	20	10	3	0	19	19	104^1	95	7	1.5	9.4	109	43%	.318
2017	ARK	AA	20	1	3	0	6	6	23^1	33	4	1.9	5.0	13	47%	.341
2018	JAX	AA	21	12	7	0	26	26	152^2	142	17	1.8	9.1	154	47%	.309
2019	JUP	A+	22	0	1	0	2	2	9^1	10	1	3.9	5.8	6	29%	.300
2019	NWO	AAA	22	3	4	0	9	9	41	45	4	4.8	8.1	37	25%	.336
2020	MIA	MLB	23	3	3	0	28	6	52	54	8	3.4	7.3	42	36%	.292

Comparables: Zach Lee, Luis Ortiz, Ronald Herrera

To reiterate that a major leaguer can be successful with the type of profile Neidert has is tired and rote: hang up a photo of Kyle Hendricks and call it a day. But Neidert offers a few wrinkles to the archetype, enough to both intrigue and befuddle. His changeup is a bit behind his other pitches in terms of its development, but in Neidert's recent AFL stint, it flashed plus. His fastball, despite sitting in the 89-91 band, has good life as Neidert can cut and run it on both sides of the plate. His breaking balls are what really shine, though, and he uses both a curve and a slider as out pitches—the former in particular can be dropped in for a strike or buried to get a hitter to chase. He'll be a candidate for the Marlins rotation as soon as 2020, but the separator between "fifth starter" and "mid-rotation stalwart" is the development of the change as more than a show-me pitch.

YEAR	TEAM	LVL	AGE	WHIP	ERA	DRA	WARP	MPH	FB%	WHF	CSP
2017	MOD	A+	20	1.07	2.76	3.40	2.3				
2017	ARK	AA	20	1.63	6.56	6.40	-0.3				
2018	JAX	AA	21	1.13	3.24	4.21	2.0				
2019	JUP	A+	22	1.50	4.82	5.38	0.0				
2019	NWO	AAA	22	1.63	5.05	5.70	0.4				
2020	MIA	MLB	23	1.40	4.63	4.89	0.4				

Sixto Sanchez RHP

Born: 07/29/98 Age: 21 Bats: R Throws: R
Height: 6'0" Weight: 185 Origin: International Free Agent, 2015

YEAR	TEAM	LVL	AGE	W	L	SV	G	GS	IP	H	HR	BB/9	K/9	K	GB%	BABIP
2017	LWD	A	18	5	3	0	13	13	67^1	46	1	1.2	8.6	64	49%	.251
2017	CLR	A+	18	0	4	0	5	5	27^2	27	1	2.9	6.5	20	42%	.295
2018	CLR	A+	19	4	3	0	8	8	46^2	39	1	2.1	8.7	45	52%	.295
2019	JUP	A+	20	0	2	0	2	2	11	14	1	1.6	4.9	6	60%	.351
2019	JAX	AA	20	8	4	0	18	18	103	87	5	1.7	8.5	97	49%	.286
2020	MIA	MLB	21	2	3	0	17	6	44	42	5	3.1	7.3	36	45%	.285

Comparables: David Holmberg, Deolis Guerra, Mike Soroka

Following a 2018 mostly lost due to elbow inflammation and a Fall League stint cut short due to collarbone discomfort, Sánchez needed a healthy, productive 2019 to convince those who aren't true believers that he can remain in a starting rotation. Sánchez responded by pumping 101 at his season debut in High-A before tossing another hundred-plus innings between there and Double-A. The stuff speaks for itself, as he continues to pair his plus-plus fastball with several good secondary pitches: His bowling ball changeup is a weapon against both righties and lefties. His slight frame may still limit his ability to be a workhorse in any rotation, but Sánchez is likely to make his major league debut as a starter in the back half of 2020. And as pitcher usage continues to mutate, his durability might not cap his no. 2 potential as much as it would have in years past.

YEAR	TEAM	LVL	AGE	WHIP	ERA	DRA	WARP	MPH	FB%	WHF	CSP
2017	LWD	A	18	0.82	2.41	2.72	2.0				
2017	CLR	A+	18	1.30	4.55	4.83	0.1				
2018	CLR	A+	19	1.07	2.51	3.48	1.0				
2019	JUP	A+	20	1.45	4.91	5.73	-0.1				
2019	JAX	AA	20	1.03	2.53	4.06	1.1				
2020	MIA	MLB	21	1.29	3.72	4.05	0.8				

LINEOUTS

Hitters

HITTER	POS	TEAM	LVL	AGE	PA	R	2B	3B	HR	RBI	BB	K	SB	CS	AVG/OBP/SLG	DRC+	WARP
Wilkin Castillo	C	NWO	AAA	35	214	23	9	2	6	24	16	30	5	1	.250/.310/.408	78	1.4
	C	MIA	MLB	35	7	0	1	0	0	2	0	3	0	0	.143/.143/.286	84	0.0
Austin Dean	LF	MIA	MLB	25	189	17	14	0	6	21	9	47	0	2	.225/.261/.404	77	-0.2
	LF	NWO	AAA	25	282	48	19	1	18	57	28	52	4	3	.337/.401/.635	148	2.6
Lewin Diaz	1B	JAX	AA	22	129	16	6	0	8	14	11	28	0	1	.200/.279/.461	122	0.5
	1B	FTM	A+	22	234	34	11	1	13	36	14	40	0	0	.290/.333/.533	157	2.0
	1B	PEN	AA	22	138	12	16	1	6	26	8	23	0	0	.302/.341/.587	130	0.9
Isaac Galloway	OF	MIA	MLB	29	54	6	1	0	0	1	0	17	2	0	.167/.167/.185	52	-0.1
	OF	NWO	AAA	29	108	19	5	0	7	16	2	41	3	1	.223/.252/.476	64	0.2
Tyler Heineman	C	NWO	AAA	28	182	26	12	2	10	25	12	21	4	0	.341/.397/.622	131	2.0
	C	MIA	MLB	28	12	1	1	0	1	2	0	4	0	0	.273/.273/.636	82	0.0
	C	RNO	AAA	28	91	16	5	1	3	13	9	14	0	0	.325/.407/.525	126	1.9
Matt Kemp	DH	CIN	MLB	34	62	4	2	0	1	5	1	19	0	0	.200/.210/.283	73	-0.2
	DH	SYR	AAA	34	36	3	0	0	1	3	2	7	0	0	.235/.278/.324	72	-0.2
Deven Marrero	3B	NWO	AAA	28	431	55	16	2	15	42	43	100	10	1	.245/.322/.415	81	1.2
	3B	MIA	MLB	28	5	0	0	0	0	0	0	3	0	0	.000/.000/.000	62	0.0
Victor Mesa Jr.	OF	MRL	Rk	17	207	39	9	4	1	24	24	29	7	4	.284/.366/.398	116	1.2
Nasim Nunez	MI	MRL	Rk	18	214	37	5	1	0	12	34	43	28	2	.211/.340/.251	88	1.2
Peter O'Brien	RF	MIA	MLB	28	47	2	1	0	1	4	4	19	1	0	.167/.255/.262	55	-0.4
	RF	NWO	AAA	28	291	41	8	0	17	45	36	107	0	1	.220/.316/.451	90	0.0
Cesar Puello	OF	LAA	MLB	28	50	6	3	0	3	12	3	8	0	0	.390/.500/.683	118	0.3
	OF	SLC	AAA	28	167	25	7	0	7	27	22	37	2	1	.296/.431/.504	112	0.2
	OF	MIA	MLB	28	97	8	2	0	1	6	7	30	0	0	.179/.281/.238	63	0.4
JT Riddle	SS	MIA	MLB	27	139	15	6	0	6	12	5	42	0	0	.189/.230/.371	69	0.0
	SS	NWO	AAA	27	131	22	10	1	4	19	6	20	3	0	.240/.277/.438	64	0.6
Yadiel Rivera	3B	NWO	AAA	27	312	38	11	1	14	46	6	81	15	6	.293/.310/.477	92	1.2
	3B	MIA	MLB	27	66	8	2	0	0	3	6	20	2	0	.183/.258/.217	59	0.0
Magneuris Sierra	CF	MIA	MLB	23	42	5	1	1	0	1	2	7	3	3	.350/.381/.425	82	0.3
	CF	JAX	AA	23	197	21	8	2	1	7	13	32	7	1	.282/.337/.365	110	1.6
	CF	NWO	AAA	23	352	56	11	7	6	21	15	58	26	10	.271/.304/.399	62	-0.3
Yangervis Solarte	3B	NWO	AAA	31	55	7	2	1	1	9	3	7	0	0	.314/.345/.451	75	-0.1
	3B	SFN	MLB	31	78	9	5	0	1	7	4	16	0	0	.205/.247/.315	65	-0.1
Chad Wallach	C	MIA	MLB	27	54	4	3	0	1	3	6	12	0	0	.250/.333/.375	96	0.2

After swearing off caffeine for a decade, **Wilkin Castillo** snagged another cup o' coffee after putting in yeoman's work for more than a half-dozen organizations and he jolted a go-ahead double in his first at-bat back for good measure. ⓧ Stare long enough at a photo of **Austin Dean** and you may start thinking he's Chris Taylor. Stare long enough at his stat line and you'll quickly be dispelled of that notion. ⓧ Three teams across two levels cashed in on **Lewin Díaz**'s materialized power in 2019, but he'll have to keep those slugging numbers afloat if he's to become a big league first sacker instead of a Quad-A disappointment. ⚾ In a story as cool as the word "rax," **Isaac Galloway** reached the majors in 2018 after more than a decade spent in the minors. Unfortunately, it looks like Galloway's big-league career will also have length in common with the word "rax." That's a verb meaning "to stretch oneself, as after sleeping," folks. Diction is important. ⚾ The defense is good and the bat has materialized enough in the minors for former UCLA catcher **Tyler Heineman**, who came over in June from the Arizona system, to hang around as a traditional type of backup. ⚾ If baseball is, at its heart, an elaborate work of symbolism, then **Matt Kemp** signing a minor-league contract with the Marlins is the most heavy-handed metaphor for death imaginable. ⚾ He still can't hit, and his sterling defense is likely to tarnish as he barrels towards his 30s, but that turn of phrase is the closest **Deven Marrero** might get to barreling anything. ⚾ With his older brother turning in a disappointing first season stateside, 17-year-old **Víctor Mesa Jr.** ditched switch-hitting and showed a penchant for getting on base as in the Gulf Coast League. ⚾ He may only stand 1.05 Altuves tall, but **Nasim Nuñez** has a great middle infielder's glove and a set of wheels—products of his agile and quick-twitch athleticism—but he'll have to hit for more power than the "absolutely none" he showed off in the Gulf Coast League if he's to be any more than a defensive replacement. ⚾ The Quad-A Corner Guy is a tried and true archetype, and **Peter O'Brien** imitates it the best he can. ⚾ Ten years in the minors and a PED suspension didn't discourage **César Puello**, who finally put up solid on-base numbers in the majors after making a career out of it in Triple-A. ⚾ **JT Riddle** is still strong enough at the six and the eight to hold a roster spot, but the stick dwindled to nigh unplayable before a forearm strain in July spelled doom for the remainder of his season. ⚾ **Yadiel Rivera** hit the upper reaches of his PECOTA projection in 2019, which meant he was exactly replacement level. ⚾ **Magneuris Sierra** rebounded slightly from an abysmal 2018 campaign, but 23-year-old outfielders who can't hit in the PCL won't get a lot of chances, even in the Marlins organization. ⚾ Even good hitters can't endure three seasons in a row of double-digit decline in DRC+, so it was especially graphic to watch this happen to **Yangervis Solarte**, who found himself forced out of the Marlins' organization as a result. ⚾ **Chad Wallach** is once again following in the footsteps of his father by playing for a team that'll be relocated soon.

Pitchers

PITCHER	TEAM	LVL	AGE	W	L	SV	G	GS	IP	H	HR	BB/9	K/9	K	GB%	WHIP	ERA	DRA	WARP
Yimi Garcia	LAN	MLB	28	1	4	0	64	0	62^1	40	15	2.0	9.5	66	30%	0.87	3.61	4.31	0.7
Jordan Holloway	JUP	A+	23	4	11	0	21	21	95	77	6	6.3	8.8	93	51%	1.51	4.45	5.74	-0.8
Tyler Kolek	CLN	A	23	0	0	0	9	0	8^1	6	0	21.6	11.9	11	25%	3.12	9.72	8.56	-0.4
Humberto Mejia	CLN	A	22	5	1	1	13	10	66^2	42	4	2.6	9.2	68	34%	0.92	2.03	2.71	1.9
	JUP	A+	22	0	1	0	5	4	23^2	15	2	1.9	8.0	21	47%	0.85	2.28	3.07	0.5
Jose Quijada	NWO	AAA	23	1	0	4	22	0	29^1	27	5	3.7	10.7	35	35%	1.33	4.30	4.07	0.6
	MIA	MLB	23	2	3	1	34	0	29^2	27	10	7.9	13.3	44	34%	1.79	5.76	5.10	0.1
Trevor Rogers	JUP	A+	21	5	8	0	18	18	110^1	97	7	2.0	10.0	122	44%	1.10	2.53	3.93	1.5
	JAX	AA	21	1	2	0	5	5	26	25	3	3.1	9.7	28	34%	1.31	4.50	4.96	0.0
Sterling Sharp	AUB	A-	24	0	1	0	2	2	7	4	0	1.3	6.4	5	76%	0.71	1.29	4.83	0.0
	HAR	AA	24	5	3	0	9	9	49^2	56	1	2.5	8.2	45	64%	1.41	3.99	5.91	-0.6
Josh Smith	PAW	AAA	31	5	3	0	13	12	67^1	82	9	2.7	9.4	70	39%	1.51	5.48	5.91	0.5
	BOS	MLB	31	0	3	1	18	2	31	36	10	2.3	8.4	29	35%	1.42	5.81	7.24	-0.6
Will Stewart	JUP	A+	21	6	12	0	23	21	129^1	137	13	2.9	6.7	96	53%	1.38	5.43	6.78	-2.8
Pat Venditte	SAC	AAA	34	6	2	0	25	1	47^1	31	5	3.2	11.2	59	34%	1.01	2.85	1.92	2.0
	SFN	MLB	34	0	0	0	2	0	3^1	4	1	5.4	5.4	2	42%	1.80	16.20	4.74	0.0
Alex Vesia	CLN	A	23	1	2	3	19	1	31^2	24	1	4.8	14.5	51	30%	1.29	2.56	3.47	0.5
	JUP	A+	23	4	0	1	10	0	18^2	12	2	0.5	11.6	24	48%	0.70	1.93	2.42	0.5
	JAX	AA	23	2	0	1	9	0	16^1	8	0	0.6	13.8	25	46%	0.55	0.00	2.62	0.4

The fan experience of watching **Yimi García** pitch is essentially playing Press Your Luck, but instead of "no whammy" everybody is desperately chanting "no homer". An otherwise fine reliever, the ding-dong problem is always lurking like the villain in a horror movie waiting for a naive individual to put him into a high-leverage spot. ⓧ Even a selection to the Florida State League All-Star Game couldn't mask **Jordan Holloway**'s unseemly 16 percent walk rate, and the 23-year-old is running out of chances to show he's deserving of a starting role. ⓧ **Tyler Kolek** finally struck out more than a third of the hitters he faced. That's good! It was as a 23-year-old in barely five innings at short-season Batavia. That's bad! ⓧ After taming the lower minors with plus control and bat-missing curve, **Humberto Mejia** will have his otherwise pedestrian repertoire tested more quickly after being added to the 40-man roster in November. ⓧ **José Quijada** is a Three True Outcomes pitcher, which for him meant that 37 percent of hits he allowed flew over the fence. ⓧ Although he isn't the sexy prospect that fellow southpaw Braxton Garrett is, **Trevor Rogers** dominated the Florida State League before a promotion to Double-A and re-joined Miami's armada of projectable arms. ⓧ **Sterling Sharp** lived up to his name with as many strikeouts as innings

Miami Marlins 2020

pitched in the Arizona Fall League, based around an on-point sinker-changeup arsenal. He'll attempt to stick with the Marlins in 2020 after being selected from Washington in the Rule 5 Draft. ⓧ Someday a few years from now when you take the "2019 Red Sox" Sporcle quiz, **Josh Smith** will be the nondescript middle reliever you can't quite recall. ⓧ When you're the fourth piece in a blockbuster trade—the third was some international bonus pool cash—you can perform as poorly as **Will Stewart** did in High-A and still see your name in this book. ⓧ On the one hand, switch-pitcher **Pat Venditte** had a marvelous year closing games for the River Cats and making a PCL All-Star Game ... but on the other hand, he had an astonishingly bad pair of appearances at the big league-level. ⓧ **Alex Vesia** started his season in the Midwest League but finished with nine scoreless appearances in Jacksonville. The former Division II starter has rapidly ascended to a true left-handed relief prospect simply by striking out everyone and walking no one. (This is only a slight exaggeration.)

Marlins Prospects

The State of the System
Hi kids, do you like upside?

The Top Ten

1. Sixto Sanchez RHP

★ ★ ★ *2020 Top 101 Prospect* **#27** ★ ★ ★

OFP: 70   ETA: 2020
Born: 07/29/98   Age: 21   Bats: R   Throws: R   Height: 6'0"   Weight: 185
Origin: International Free Agent, 2015

The Report: If you are one of the top pitching prospects in all of baseball, the cornerstone trade return for arguably the best catcher in the game, and having just finished the season injury-free in Double-A, you should feel pretty good, right? If you're Sixto Sanchez, there is plenty to be excited about, yet some prominent questions remain as the scrutiny of the big leagues looms.

Standing just 6-foot even, Sanchez is unquestionably blessed with a power arm that few others his stature can feature. Routinely running it up into the high-90s and above, he uses a stout lower half in his delivery to generate extra velocity as he torques over his front hip. The fastball is, well, fast. However, it lacks complementary life, movement, and finish despite its elite velocity. While his command is better than you'd expect from a generic triple-digit fireballer—if such a thing exists—it's not a pitch he consistently controls in the zone.

The secondaries are good—not great—with the ability to throw off the timing of the hitter if he tries to cheat on the heater. The slider is short and snappy, used primarily to the glove-side where it breaks more, as opposed to flattening out on the arm-side. His changeup took a big step forward in 2019, touching 90 regularly with good sinking action as it approaches the plate. But neither the slider nor the changeup are formidable punch-out pitches.

With the straightness of the fastball, Sanchez has had to rely more on getting outs in the field than someone of his pedigree. Of the pitchers listed in our midseason top 50, and the rough draft of our forthcoming Top 101, nobody has a lower strikeout percentage than Sanchez. Given his injury history, diminutive size, low walks (good) and low strikeouts (bad), you have to begin to wonder if his future is destined for an electric late-inning relief role.

Variance: Extreme. This can go any number of directions. He could be a No. 2 or 3 starter, he could be a high-leverage reliever, he could be a star when healthy or have his playing time cut short. Such is the life of a 21-year-old who throws really hard and doesn't have a long track record of sustained success.

Mark Barry's Fantasy Take: Please don't tell any of my bosses, but for some reason I'm lukewarm on Sixto. For a guy with triple-digit heat and one-and-a-half plus secondaries, it really feels like he should strike more dudes out. Seeing Sanchez eclipse the 100-inning mark for the first time is certainly encouraging, but he has yet to punch out a batter per inning at any level, despite premium stuff. I'm obviously not saying Sanchez is bad, far from it, but I am concerned about his trajectory into fantasy acedom.

★ ★ ★ *2020 Top 101 Prospect* **#35** ★ ★ ★

2

JJ Bleday OF   OFP: 60   ETA: 2021
Born: 11/10/97   Age: 22   Bats: L   Throws: L   Height: 6'3"   Weight: 205
Origin: Round 1, 2019 Draft (#4 overall)

The Report: Bleday is not the most exciting 2019 draftee to write about. Adley Rutschman could be a generational catching prospect, Andrew Vaughn might be the best pure bat we've seen in a bit, and Bobby Witt, Riley Greene and CJ Abrams—to name three—arguably have more upside. Bleday is merely a very good, polished, college corner outfielder. He's got more than enough arm for right field and should be above-average there, but man that is not an exciting lede for the fourth-overall pick in the draft. Frankly the lede has been buried here already, so let's dig up, stupid. While Vaughn might be the best pure bat in this year's draft class, Bleday isn't that far behind. He actually lapped Vaughn on game power his junior year, swatting 26 home runs for Vanderbilt. This was an important development for Bleday, who was on follow lists for a while due to his hitting ability and power potential, but it wasn't until last summer on the Cape that he started dragging that plus pop into games. Now he's a potential plus hit/plus power right fielder who could move quickly—the Marlins sent him to the Florida State League right out of the draft—and he has a relatively high floor. There's plus bat speed and good strength out of his broad, athletic frame. He has a solid command of the strike zone and enough barrel control to flick a base hit if he gets fooled. Bleday might not have the most upside in the 2019 draft class, but he's very likely to be somewhere in the middle of the lineup on the next good Marlins team.

Variance: Medium. We think he will hit, but with a corner outfield profile, he'll need to really hit to be a plus regular.

Mark Barry's Fantasy Take: As it turns out, folding a little power into an already strong offensive profile is, uh, good. Bleday smashed 26 homers and slugged over .700 as a junior at Vanderbilt before heading straight to High-A after the draft. The power retention will dictate his ceiling, but if some version of the breakout sticks, Bleday has OF2 upside.

─────── ★ ★ ★ *2020 Top 101 Prospect* **#52** ★ ★ ★ ───────

3
Jazz Chisholm SS   OFP: 60   ETA: 2021
Born: 02/01/98   Age: 22   Bats: L   Throws: R   Height: 5'11"   Weight: 165
Origin: International Free Agent, 2015

The Report: Another top prospect brought in from outside the organization, Chisholm was a breakout name after a dominant 2018 season that had him slashing .272/.329/.513 with 25 dingers between two levels of A-ball. Yes, there were strikeouts. In fact, there were a lot of them. But with that kind of offensive production, as well as plus athleticism with commensurate defensive ability, it was worth overlooking all the whiffs.

That is, until the first half of 2019 where he struckout 85 times in 59 games at Double-A Jackson and saw his batting average dip below .200 until the Fourth of July. The power was still present, as Chisholm jacked 13 homers in a notoriously difficult hitting environment. He also swiped a handful of bases, and improved his walk rate compared to prior years. With those tools still present, Arizona and Miami pulled off a rare double-prospect trade.

Chisholm was largely the same player in the final month of the season with his new organization, with slightly fewer strikeouts that will hopefully provide some distance from the projection of a rare non-first-base/DH Three True Outcomes offensive player. He is a dynamic, quick-twitch player that you can tell is having fun when out on the diamond. If the approach can continue to tighten up, he can be one of the better all-around middle infield prospects in the game.

Variance: Very high. It all boils down to how much will he strikeout. Because he will strikeout; probably a lot. If it's down closer to 25 percent of the time, it will be overshadowed by the damage inflicted with the bat.

Mark Barry's Fantasy Take: Because I'm ever the rosy optimist, let's start with the good: Jazz hit 21 dingers and snagged 16 bags in 2019, while drawing walks over 11 percent of the time. The bad: there were strikeouts, oh so many strikeouts. Chisholm could be a 20/20 guy, a feat only nine big leaguers achieved in 2019, but there's substantial risk that he'll strike out too much to reach that upside. He's a top-50 guy still, but the variance is immense.

─────── ★ ★ ★ *2020 Top 101 Prospect* **#80** ★ ★ ★ ───────

4
Jesús Sánchez OF   OFP: 60   ETA: 2021
Born: 10/07/97   Age: 22   Bats: L   Throws: R   Height: 6'3"   Weight: 230
Origin: International Free Agent, 2014

The Report: Selling high on a lofty reliever and depth starter, the Marlins were able to nab quite the haul in Jesús Sánchez from Tampa in their midseason trade. At every stop in his professional matriculation up the Rays organization, Sánchez did nothing but hit for high average year after year. The questions were—and still are to some degree—is the hit tool sustainable, and will the power develop?

It's a compact setup that relies on his excellent hands and barrel control to meet the ball, casting the bat instead of engaging his core to invoke more power. The bat-speed isn't elite, which leads evaluators to wonder whether his strength gains will help turn more doubles into home runs. One positive trend, despite lackluster numbers in Triple-A, is his propensity to adapt to a level change. Even after struggles, he's shown an ability to learn and improve, coming back better the second time around. It stems from a desire to compete which is evident in every at-bat: he wants to beat you.

So much of the projection is reliant upon the offensive upside, but he's also an average runner and won't hurt you in the field, featuring a strong arm perfectly suited for right field. If for some reason the stick never fulfills its full potential, he's at worst a very good option off the bench. At best? He's a corner outfielder with middle of the order run production attributes.

Variance: High. He could be an All-Star, he really could. But there is a plateau effect in play, that if you keep thinking something will happen in development and it hasn't yet, you wonder if it ever will.

Mark Barry's Fantasy Take: Sánchez was better after changing Florida zip codes at the deadline, but still hasn't lived up to the promise of his breakout 2017 campaign. His proximity to the big club keeps him in the dynasty consciousness, but he still needs some work offensively to be better than an OF5.

★ ★ ★ *2020 Top 101 Prospect* **#97** ★ ★ ★

5 **Edward Cabrera** **RHP** OFP: 55 ETA: 2021
Born: 04/13/98 Age: 22 Bats: R Throws: R Height: 6'4" Weight: 175
Origin: International Free Agent, 2015

The Report: Cabrera had a breakout campaign in 2019, adding improved command to his plus-plus velocity. His fastball sat at 94-96 and touched 100 several times. He has good feel for spinning his curve, though the movement can still be inconsistent. Cabrera improved his change this season, and it now has the potential to be a third above-average pitch. He mixes his pitches well and can keep hitters off-balance with changes in velocity and movement.

The biggest challenge for Cabrera going forward is to continue to refine the secondary stuff and command, and to prove he can handle a starter's workload, as he has never thrown more than 100 1/3 innings in a season. That's not uncommon for a young pitcher moving quickly through the minors, it does increase the risk factor. But the improvements Cabrera showed in 2019 were uniformly positive markers.

Variance: Medium. Durability and stamina concerns remain, but the stuff is starter-quality, and he has some Double-A success under his belt.

Mark Barry's Fantasy Take: It must be nice adding around 10 percentage points to your strikeout rate as you ascend through the system as Cabrera did in 2019. If this trend continues, Cabrera could be punching out 100 percent of batters by 2027. For real, though, Cabrera is a legit dude, with the potential to have the "D" capitalized. I'd have him in the top-150, and he could even flirt with the top-100.

6 Monte Harrison   OF   OFP: 55   ETA: 2020
Born: 08/10/95   Age: 24   Bats: R   Throws: R   Height: 6'3"   Weight: 220
Origin: Round 2, 2014 Draft (#50 overall)

The Report: Harrison missed a bunch of time this year with a wrist injury that required some summer surgery, but overall he bounced back some from a poor 2018 campaign in Double-A. He's tinkered with his setup and swing during his recent pro struggles, but seems to have returned to a similar setup and the small leg lift that he employed during his 2017 breakout. He's filled out some in the lower half, but it's still a very athletic, high-waisted frame.

Harrison still looks the part of a five-tool center fielder. The bat doesn't look quite as quick and whippy as it once did, and his feel for spin can remain raw, but the hand-eye is good enough to project an average hit tool, which should allow enough of the raw power to manifest in games to give him a shot to be an outfield regular. That hit tool is still projection-heavy for a guy in Triple-A, though.

Harrison glides out there in center, and he's improved his reads and routes enough that he's not just getting by on pure foot speed. He could use some more consolidation time in Triple-A, and while he's older now than you might think—he turned 24 at the end of last season—the upside remains tantalizing. However, it's now more in the mold of a solid power/speed everyday outfielder, not quite the same all-star heights we dreamt of after 2017.

Variance: High. You know the drill by now. The swing-and-miss here could lead to a lot of hit tool variance. See Lewis Brinson or Isan Díaz's issues in the majors so far (the Marlins sure have a type). On the other hand, all five tools still pop up from time to time, and if he comes back from his wrist injury in 2020 without issue, it's still a profile I'd like to bet on.

Mark Barry's Fantasy Take: Harrison swiped 23 bags in 25 tries this season, a mix of speed and skill that portends well for his future in base thievery. That alone keeps him in the top-100 or so, and his proximity to the big leagues probably has him closer to the top-50. The strikeouts are concerning and have always been Harrison's biggest obstacle irl and in fantasy, keeping his range of outcomes wide.

Miami Marlins 2020

7 **Jorge Guzman   RHP**   OFP: 55   ETA: Late 2020
Born: 01/28/96   Age: 24   Bats: R   Throws: R   Height: 6'2"   Weight: 182
Origin: International Free Agent, 2014

The Report: There is a lot to like about Guzman. He has a plus fastball that sits 95-97 and occasionally hits triple digits. His slider and change both flash above average. But that makes him just about every decent pitching prospect nowadays. Guzman's failure to rise above the crowd is largely due to his inability to consistently repeat his delivery. The resulting command issues have hounded him throughout his career, and though there were hints of improvement at times in 2019, it is looking more and more like a relief profile long-term. The good news is that it should be a high-leverage role as the fastball is definitely a weapon. A move to the pen would allow Guzman to focus on just his change as the only secondary pitch he would need. That pitch improved over the course of the season and could develop into a swing-and-miss offering. It's time for the Marlins to make Guzman a reliever and let him help in Miami quickly.

Variance: High. There remains significant relief risk here and the command might make him just a frustrating and tantalizing setup guy.

Mark Barry's Fantasy Take: As Bret mentioned in Guzman's write up from last season, the former Yankee prospect still has more name value than fantasy value, mostly due to him being, well, a former Yankee prospect. The stuff still dazzles in flashes, but for me the control is spotty enough to keep him outside the top-200.

8 **Lewin Diaz   1B**   OFP: 55   ETA: 2021
Born: 11/19/96   Age: 23   Bats: L   Throws: L   Height: 6'4"   Weight: 225
Origin: International Free Agent, 2013

The Report: Diaz was acquired for Sergio Romo in the midst of what was a breakout season for him in the Twins organization. He has plus raw power and his swing is becoming more efficient in translating that to games. He starts with his hands low and he generates good loft and bat speed. He also shows a rapidly-improving hit tool, with good pitch recognition. He can effectively use the whole field and he makes a lot of contact for a power hitter. Diaz has worked to make himself a good player defensively. He has good hands and range and improving footwork around the bag. The development needs to continue as the margins on this profile are razor-thin, but Diaz seems like the perfect addition to a system that had been very pitcher-heavy.

Variance: Medium. The progression of power development could break down at any time and/or the hit tool could disappear into the power-sellout vortex.

Mark Barry's Fantasy Take: I'm a big fan of this guy, especially the way he walked around in the cold with the cat and, like, sang folk songs and stuff. I don't know, I kind of fell asleep during that one. Aside from his vocals, Diaz has some budding pop, which is cool, but is otherwise a 1B-only prospect in the NL, which means those budding skills will have to bloom in a big way for him to be fantasy useful.

9. Trevor Rogers LHP OFP: 55 ETA: 2021
Born: 11/13/97 Age: 22 Bats: L Throws: L Height: 6'6" Weight: 185
Origin: Round 1, 2017 Draft (#13 overall)

The Report: Depending on who you asked before the 2017 draft, Trevor Rogers fell somewhere in the 25-50 range of best available players, yet was selected 13th overall by Miami. Ignoring the competition level of rural New Mexico, his older draft age as a high schooler—and a very scrawny 6-foot-6 frame—his selection was considered somewhat surprising at the time. After a breakout 2019 campaign, most detractors have been silenced.

The tall lefty is all arms and legs, utilizing those long levers in a surprisingly repeatable delivery that has good tempo. Spotting to either corner of the plate, the fastball has late arm-side finish in the low-90s, bumping as high as 95 when needed. The breaking ball is a tad slurvy with side-to-side break but flashes plus when thrown in the lower 80s. And his changeup shows good feel and depth that, with more consistency, could be another plus offering.

With a late season taste of Double-A in just his second full season as a pro, Rogers will likely remain in the Southern League for most of 2020 for further maturation, yet his trajectory is certainly trending upwards.

Variance: High. From both an evaluation and statistical standpoints, Rogers has done everything and more in his first two full years. Even with a "high" risk that comes with a young pitcher, it's a fairly mild risk given his ability to log innings at an advanced rate for his experience.

Mark Barry's Fantasy Take: Rogers could be a decent starting pitcher occupying the middle or back-end of a rotation. That's good for a real-life baseball club, but it's less good for dynasty leagues.

10. Kameron Misner OF OFP: 55 ETA: 2023
Born: 01/08/98 Age: 22 Bats: L Throws: L Height: 6'4" Weight: 219
Origin: Round 1, 2019 Draft (#35 overall)

The Report: Misner possesses an extra-large frame, lean muscle, and displays tons of athleticism with plus speed. There is true five-tool potential here. At the plate, he employs a short and quick stroke with a fairly flat bat path. The lefty rarely expands the zone and owns a patient, selective approach. During batting practice, he shows plenty of power, but mainly to the pull side. Misner can spray it line-to-line, just not for round-trippers yet. When he finds a gap, his wheels take over. His ability to regularly swipe bags highlight plus instincts on the basepaths. He profiles as an above-average center fielder down the road. Coming in on fly balls is Misner's strength, but he can improve on going back to the wall and getting quicker jumps. He has outstanding body control, and exhibits great footwork to gather himself to make strong throws, an easy plus arm in any situation. It seems as though Misner is a more polished—with a higher ceiling—version of Connor Scott.

Variance: High. The only real concern is translating his raw power into games. Even if power doesn't come, he still has four plus tools to work with, but then he falls into the mold of every typical center fielder.

Mark Barry's Fantasy Take: How lucky do you feel? Misner is an uber-athlete with 25/25 upside and a great patience at the dish. His floor feels poor-man's Jake Marisnick-y, however, which is far less appealing.

The Next Ten

11 **Braxton Garrett   LHP**
Born: 08/05/97   Age: 22   Bats: L   Throws: L   Height: 6'3"   Weight: 190
Origin: Round 1, 2016 Draft (#7 overall)

Having nearly fully recovered from Tommy John surgery that cost him all of 2018, Garrett had a big bounce-back year in 2019, pitching well enough in High-A to eclipse the 100-inning mark and earning a final start to the season in Double-A. Following surgery, velocity is typically the first to return after strength rehab, and command typically the last thing to develop. While not to be confused as a hard-thrower pre-surgery, Garrett struck out over a batter an inning and kept modest walk totals. The fastball velocity for both the two-seamer and four-seamer with natural cut, seems to be a tick down, but it's balanced out by a very good curveball.

The hammer curve was its usual self, showing good 12-6 finish. Garrett can throw the hook in any count with abundant confidence. The changeup is still lagging behind, while fastball command is coming along, but given the low expectations for the former first round pick for this season, his successes were a welcome sight as he heads into what should be a fully healthy 2020 campaign. It will be interesting to see what off-season strength gains have been made, and whether the kid-gloves will be off for the next step of development.

12 **Víctor Víctor Mesa   OF**
Born: 07/20/96   Age: 23   Bats: R   Throws: R   Height: 5'10"   Weight: 165
Origin: International Free Agent, 2018

Craig recently asked me if Mesa was the biggest one-year drop for a team number one prospect. I don't really have the time to research it right now, Craig, but I can try to contextualize it. Mainly, it's a set of circumstances which are unlikely to reoccur. Mesa was a soft number one in a shallow system last year, and he'd have been unseated by Sixto if that trade hadn't happened just after the Futures Guide cutoff. We also had far less info on him than I'd like when ranking a prospect at the top of a system. Mesa hadn't played any sort of pro baseball in over a year, and was more akin to a top dollar J2 IFA, who I would tend to be more conservative with in terms of ranking. But he was 21, not 16, the reports were good, and the Serie Nacional ain't the Dominican showcase circuit.

But we do have a lot more information now. Last year's Almora comp looks about right on the glove and speed, and less so on the bat...well, actually Almora was pretty bad last year wasn't he? Maybe it still works offensively too, but comping 2019 Albert Almora is not what you want. Mesa is already a major league quality center fielder, with an arm that will play in any outfield spot, and he's a plus baserunner. However, he has struggled to make quality contact in his first year in pro ball, and hasn't looked the part at the plate at all. Mesa deserves (and needs) time to adjust, but the profile here looks more bench outfielder than starter at present.

13 Nick Neidert RHP
Born: 11/20/96 Age: 23 Bats: R Throws: R Height: 6'1" Weight: 202
Origin: Round 2, 2015 Draft (#60 overall)

We usually associate prospect fatigue with top prospects we've just run out of things to say about to the point where it a prime example. But it can strike lesser prospects as well. This is the fifth time we've included Neidert on a team list at Baseball Prospectus. He went from a backend starting pitching prospect in a bad Mariners system, to a backend starting pitching prospect in a bad Marlins system, to a backend starting pitching prospect in a much-improved Marlins system. The organizational improvements around him account for much of his slide down the list since last year, although he did miss significant time in 2019 with knee tendinitis.

When he was on the mound he was still extremely Nick Neidert. A low-90s fastball with enough movement and command to play a tick above-average. The changeup is clearly above-average with plus sinking action and good arm speed. Neither breaking ball is anything to write home about—or a blurb about, but he throws strikes with everything. Everything can also be a bit too hittable in the zone. This is rarely a profile that excites me, the 90-mph, good-change righty. But Neidert has a little bit better fastball command and a little bit better change than the average member of this not-very-exclusive club. I'm still not sold that he's much more than a backend/swing type, but I have now conjured enough words to fight off the fatigue for one more list cycle.

14 Jose Devers IF
Born: 12/07/99 Age: 20 Bats: L Throws: R Height: 6'0" Weight: 155
Origin: International Free Agent, 2016

Part of the Marlins' return in exchange for Giancarlo Stanton, Devers was known mostly for his glove at the time of the trade. He's still an above-average defender at the six. Fluid and athletic, he has soft hands and shows a natural feel in the field. The bat, formerly an afterthought, took a major step forward last season as Devers held his own as a teenager in the Florida State League. The swing is geared for line drives and he shows an above-average ability to make contact. There's also a discipline in his approach which is rare in younger players as he controls the zone and recognizes spin well. He is never going to hit for much power but the trifecta of hit tool, speed, and defense give him a pretty high floor. Another strong year of offensive development and Devers could be a fast mover in the organization.

15 **Connor Scott OF**
Born: 10/08/99   Age: 20   Bats: L   Throws: L   Height: 6'4"   Weight: 180
Origin: Round 1, 2018 Draft (#13 overall)

A first-round selection in 2018, Scott has an athletic, tall and lean frame. So far in his pro career, he's impressed more with his defense than his bat. Playing center field, the lefty shows plus range in every direction, while taking efficient routes to the ball. Scott also displays a natural feel and smoothness for the position. The arm strength is plus with an easy throwing motion. At the plate Scott's disciplined and patient approach helps him control the zone well. However, he doesn't have the quickest bat and struggles to barrel inside fastballs on occasion. He also lacks consistent over-the-fence power, but is strong enough to run in to a few. His plus wheels do make him an extra- and stolen-base threat, although his running technique is odd with very long strides and arms that flail out. The defense and speed give Scott a higher floor, but his ceiling is limited because of his offensive profile. He will need to make more consistent hard contact to swim with the fish in Miami.

16 **Jerar Encarnacion OF**
Born: 10/22/97   Age: 22   Bats: R   Throws: R   Height: 6'4"   Weight: 219
Origin: International Free Agent, 2015

You'll be hard-pressed to find a bigger internal development success story for the Marlins than Encarnacion. As an 18-year-old signee out of the Dominican, little had been accomplished in his career prior to 2019 with only two facts being aboundingly clear: he was big and strong. The 6-foot-4 masher destroyed the Midwest League in the first half of the season, hitting .298/.363/.478 with 10 bombs, promptly earning a promotion to High-A. The batting stance elicits memories of former Marlins slugger Giancarlo Stanton, closing his front-side off at delivery to keep his shoulder inside the ball before uncorking a powerful hip pivot that explodes the bat through the zone. He isn't the most fleet of foot, so he may not be long for the outfield, likely ending up at first base. After a strong showing in the Arizona Fall League—including a grand slam in the championship game—Encarnacion will attempt to follow up in 2020 with an equally impressive year; a welcome sight for the higher-ups that want to see more right-handed power in their system.

17   Alex Vesia   LHP
Born: 04/11/96   Age: 24   Bats: L   Throws: L   Height: 6'2"   Weight: 195
Origin: Round 17, 2018 Draft (#507 overall)

When last draft's 17th-round senior sign out of Cal State-East Bay—the Pioneers, if you were wondering—makes your prospect list, it usually means one of two things: 1) You have a very, very bad system, like late 00's Astros bad, or 2) you pulled off a very nice bit of draft and development work. Vesia is the latter. The fastball velocity is only average, but emerges from a deceptive arm action and a high slot, while generating plenty of sink to keep the heater off of barrels. He commands the fastball well east-west, and it plays up to above-average from the left side. He pairs it with a mid-80s slider that he can manipulate to either side of the plate. It will flash plus with late depth when he wants to come in with it against righties and is good enough to crossover, given how well he commands it generally. There's a change for a different look against righties, too, although it acts more like a firm two-seamer. Vesia goes right after hitters, but the stuff and command make him no mere minor league southpaw strike-thrower who gets found out when you add on the third deck. The upside here isn't huge, but Vesia is a quality relief prospect.

18   Jordan Holloway   RHP
Born: 06/13/96   Age: 24   Bats: R   Throws: R   Height: 6'6"   Weight: 215
Origin: Round 20, 2014 Draft (#587 overall)

Selected as a physically projectable right-hander in the 20th round of the 2014 draft, it has been a rough road to present day for the power arm from Colorado. He missed the second half of 2017 and all of 2018 after Tommy John surgery. Despite the missed time, he was protected from the Rule 5 draft and added to the 40-man roster last year, showing just how much the Miami brass believed in the talent. His live arm was back in full effect for 2019, but so were some of the command problems that plagued him prior to his surgery. The profile has far more upside as a reliever, where he can sit in the upper-90s and touch 100, while featuring a power breaker as a true swing-and-miss pitch.

19   Nasim Nunez   SS
Born: 08/18/00   Age: 19   Bats: B   Throws: R   Height: 5'9"   Weight: 160
Origin: Round 2, 2019 Draft (#46 overall)

Nunez—the Marlins second-round pick this past summer—lacks for some present strength or physical projection, but he's a polished, quick-twitch shortstop, who should not only stick at the 6, but be above-average there. He's athletic and rangy in the field, with a plus arm that can make all the throws. He's a plus-plus runner down the line, and the speed will be a weapon on the basepaths. There's good markers in the hit tool here too, as Nunez has a loose, line drive swing with good feel for the barrel considering his age and limited pro experience. The main question on the offensive side is whether he will be strong enough to keep the bat from getting knocked out of his hands against better velocity up the ladder. The speed and defensive tools should earn him a bench role regardless, but if he can show some sting in the bat when he sees 95+, he could carve out a starting role as a tablesetter type.

20   Robert Dugger   RHP
Born: 07/03/95   Age: 24   Bats: R   Throws: R   Height: 6'2"   Weight: 180
Origin: Round 18, 2016 Draft (#537 overall)

When you get down to the 24-year-old, 20th prospect on the team, you kind of know what the description will be. Duggar handled Double-A hitters pretty well with a repertoire that can best be described as average. His fastball rarely topped 90 and he had no standout secondary pitches. He did it all with decent command and an understanding of his craft. He mixed pitches, changed speeds, changed eye levels and kept inexperienced hitters off balance. Then he went to Triple-A and, later, to the major leagues. It didn't work quite as well at those levels. Fly-ball pitchers without overpowering stuff do not find a friend in the Triple-A/MLB baseball and Dugger was no exception. There is still time for him to figure out how he can pitch effectively at the upper levels, but the likely outcome is looking like an up-and-down starter or long reliever.

Personal Cheeseball

PC   Evan Edwards   1B
Born: 06/21/97   Age: 23   Bats: L   Throws: L   Height: 6'0"   Weight: 200
Origin: Round 4, 2019 Draft (#111 overall)

Okay, so 6-foot, left/left first basemen and I have a bit of a checkered history. It's not my favorite profile. And while Edwards is stout, even bordering on rectangular of frame, he is not yet a big enough boy to pique Wilson's interest. He does have a quality beard, actually paying attention to shape and lines without being overly finicky about it, a rarity among baseball players. He has big forearms, the whole aesthetics of the look just work with the profile. And the profile isn't that bad. I could easily slip Edwards into the Low Minors Sleeper spot as well. He's aggressive and swings hard. There's some stiffness as well, and he may never make enough contact to consistently get his power from those forearms into games, but it's intriguing pop and he's a very good defender at first base. A defense-first, shorter first baseman with bat questions. Yeah, not exactly filling out a bingo card of my predilections here, but sometimes you surprise yourself.

Low Minors Sleeper

LMS

Will Banfield C
Born: 11/18/99 Age: 20 Bats: R Throws: R Height: 6'0" Weight: 200
Origin: Round 2, 2018 Draft (#69 overall)

The Midwest League is an aggressive assignment for a prep catcher, even for one that was a second-round pick. His long swing was overmatched by full-season stuff, and while there's some power in the profile, Banfield will need a lot of refinement at the dish to tap into it. The picture is brighter on the defensive side. He's built like a catcher, with a sturdy but athletic frame. He blocks well, he has a cannon for an arm, and projects well as a receiver. He's going to have to hit some to make the majors, but there's the outline of a catch-and-throw backup with some pop already, and he was only 19 in Clinton last year.

Top Talents 25 and Under (as of 4/1/2020)

1. Sixto Sanchez
2. JJ Bleday
3. Sandy Alcantara
4. Jazz Chisholm
5. Jesús Sánchez
6. Isan Díaz
7. Jordan Yamamoto
8. Edward Cabrera
9. Monte Harrison
10. Jorge Guzman

Alcantara threw 197 1/3 innings with a 3.88 ERA and a 45 percent groundball rate in his first extended look at major-league action. He threw two complete game shutouts. He also had games where he struggled to complete five innings and couldn't find the plate. All told, he was a 2.6-WARP pitcher who looked the part of a mid-rotation workhorse who does just enough to stick around but not enough to anchor a rotation. That's great, but doesn't quite trump the upside of the likes of Sanchez and Bleday. In conclusion, Alcantara is a pitcher of contrasts. The only two other players on the list who exhausted their prospect eligibility are Díaz and Yamamoto. Díaz checked in at No. 4 in the system a year ago and laid waste to the PCL to earn an August call-up, after which he struggled mightily. He still projects to have above-average pop and can hold his own at second, the question is if the hit tool and plate discipline come around to the point where the profile isn't entirely reliant on him hitting bombs. 30+ homers with no OBP doesn't buy what it used to. Yamamoto made the jump from Double-A to the majors in June and found himself with a Jacob deGrom-ian 1.59 ERA through his first six starts. He regressed as expected, but a DRA of 3.56 says he was actually significantly better than the 4.46 ERA. His upside is somewhere in the No. 3 or 4 starter range, but that's not too shabby for the fourth piece in the now-infamous Christian Yelich trade.

Part 3: Featured Articles

The Baseball Is Juiced (Again)

Robert Arthur

This article originally appeared at Baseball Prospectus on April 5, 2019.

It started when the normally reliable Chris Sale got lit up for three homers by the Mariners in the Red Sox's season opener. It was part of a record number of taters that flew on Opening Day, as starters from Sale to Zack Greinke were taken deep by the handful. Then Christian Yelich hit a home run in each of his first four games, tying yet another MLB record, this one for consecutive games with a dinger to start a season.

It didn't take long for fans and players to begin whispering and tweeting about the baseballs being juiced again. It's early yet for us to come to any definitive conclusion about the 2019 season, but preliminary data shows that the baseball has returned to its aerodynamic peak. Whether that means this season will smash home run records like 2017 did remains to be seen.

Before home run explosion over the last few years, no one worried too much about the baseball's air resistance. While MLB and Rawlings (the company that manufactures the official baseballs) kept track of dozens of metrics to make sure that the ball was consistent from month to month, they didn't measure drag.

But drag is incredibly important in determining how likely a hitter is to knock one out of the park. As baseballs become more aerodynamic, they travel further given a certain initial velocity. A deep fly ball that might have been caught at the warning track can instead go into the first row of the stands. A three percent change in drag coefficient can work to add about five feet to a well-hit fly ball, which can in turn increase home runs league wide by an astounding 10-15 percent.

It's possible to measure the aerodynamics of the baseball using the pitch-tracking radars currently in place in each MLB ballpark. By calculating the loss of speed from when the pitch is released to when it crosses the plate, you can directly measure the drag coefficient on the baseball. I first wrote about the role of decreasing drag in boosting home runs in 2017, and MLB's commission of scientists and statisticians later confirmed that the more aerodynamic baseballs in use that year were largely to blame for the spike in home runs. The same commission rejected some alternate hypotheses, like rising temperatures and a league-wide boost in launch angle pushing more balls over the fence.

The current era has featured some large fluctuations in drag coefficient, leading to first an explosion in 2016 and 2017, and then a dialing back of homers last year. Curious about the record-breaking home run tallies in the last few days, I used the same methodology to measure the aerodynamics of the baseballs so far in 2019.

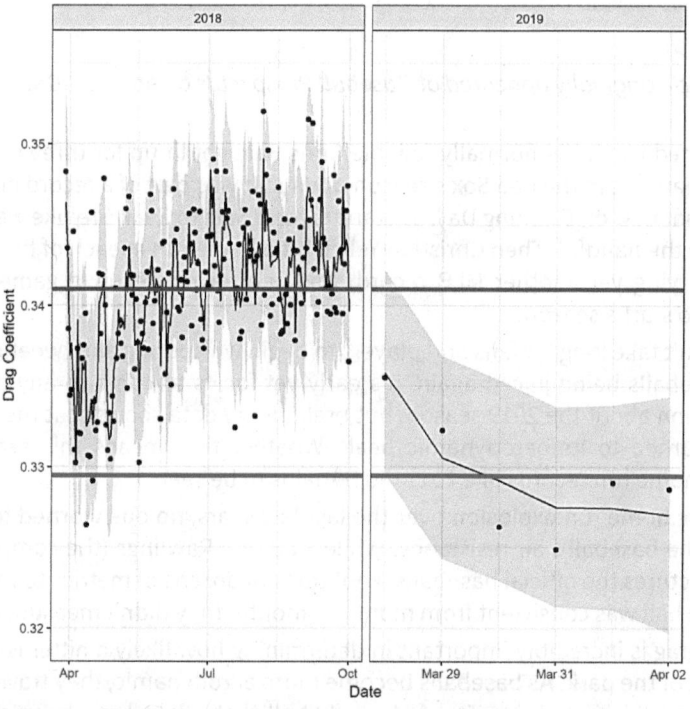

We're only a week into the 2019 season, but the drag numbers so far are among the lowest recorded in the last calendar year. With apologies for gory math, the current 2019 season average drag coefficient (the red line) would be below the 95 percent credible interval (the shaded area) for about nine-tenths of the 2018 season. (I used a Bayesian Random Walk model implemented in INLA to calculate these credible intervals, averaging the drag numbers in each game and adjusting for park.)

There were only a handful of six-day stretches in 2018 that had drag numbers below what we're seeing now, and most were in late June and early July. All of this means that 2019's data so far is quite a bit different than what we saw through most of last year.

These drag coefficients factor out the effects of temperature and air density, so they aren't a product of April cold. However, the numbers could be deceptive if the radars used to track pitches have changed from year to year. I consulted with some experts within baseball who were not aware of any specific modifications to the radar this year that could produce this pattern, but it's an important caveat of which to be aware.

On the one hand, it's only been six days, and we don't quite have the statistical basis to say that these drag coefficients are unprecedented compared to 2018. On the other hand, we've witnessed about 5,000 fastballs so far this season, so it's not as if our sample size is small. At least so far, the baseball has played like it's much more aerodynamic than it was last year. In fact, the current drag coefficient is really only comparable to 2017, when the baseballs were more aerodynamic than they had been in at least a decade.

It's not just fancy radar tracking indicating that the baseball is flying through the air more easily. The current number of home runs per game (as of this writing) is the highest it's been since the heady days of 2017, the year that teams and players broke dinger-related records everywhere you looked. That's especially remarkable considering that we're in what is typically the coldest part of the regular season, when lower temperatures and higher winds tend to suppress offense and keep balls in the air within the park. Comparing only from April to April, this year's rate of home runs per fly ball is even a little bit higher than it was in 2017.

With that said, the current measurements are no guarantee that 2019 will be another year of record-shattering homer hitting. The trouble with the drag measurements is that they are not consistent from June to August, from week to week, or even sometimes from day to day. Whether because of natural manufacturing variation or differences in the underlying supplies of cowhide and thread that go into the baseballs, drag has a tendency to fluctuate up and down over the course of a year. So the homers that fly in the first week of April wouldn't necessarily clear the fence a week later.

It's possible that this one-week drop in drag coefficient subsides and the baseball returns to its 2018 levels. On the other hand, it's almost equally probable that the ball becomes even more slippery and flies ever farther. Either way, it's clear that the baseball's air resistance is something to keep an eye on for the remainder of the 2019 season.

—*Robert Arthur is an author of Baseball Prospectus.*

The Moral Hazard of Playing It Safe

Craig Goldstein

This article originally appeared at Baseball Prospectus on August 6, 2019.

A couple days prior to the trade deadline, amidst a sea of tranquility posing as the lead up to the trade deadline, Bob Nightengale took to Twitter. Nightengale, who was probably wearing his pants backwards at the time, tweeted that MLB GMs were coming around on the idea that the unified trade deadline should be moved back from July 31 to August 15, so they could better assess their positions in the standings and whether they should buy or sell. To which I said:

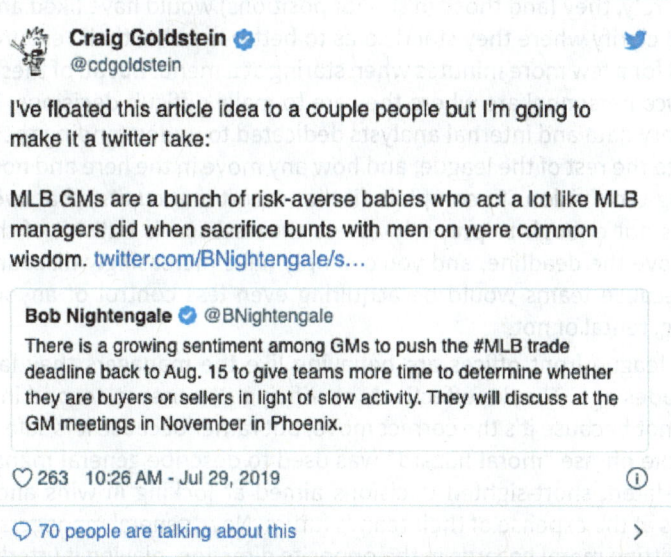

This might strike some as reductive and churlish. And it might be that, but it isn't really wrong, either. Jeff Quinton wrote a great piece discussing the environmental factors that enable front offices to avoid risk without upsetting the apple cart within their own fanbases. I don't believe that it goes far enough, however. His article gives us the proper framework through which to understand why these behaviors have been allowed to seep into front offices throughout the league. Understanding the reasons behind these actions are different from excusing them, though, and GMs should not be let off the hook for their non-competitive approach to the trade deadline (much less the offseason).

⚾ ⚾ ⚾

It's fair to say that fans as a group have rarely, if ever, been pro-player. It is also fair to say that in the time during and following the Moneyball revolution, the pendulum swung from fans who cared intensely about winning in the moment (and thus might be intolerant of a rebuilding approach) to fans who supported building a team that could compete throughout multiple seasons, viewing the playoffs as a crapshoot, with the thought that getting multiple bites at the apple was a better approach than taking a bigger bite in any one season.

There's nothing wrong with that approach, and I still find merit in that argument. However, it seems that the pendulum has swung too far in that direction. Teams are overvaluing some of the individual factors that make themselves long-term contenders rather than attempting to seize a championship when given the opportunity. It's a difficult needle to thread.

And surely, they (and those in similar positions) would have liked another two weeks to clarify where they stand so as to better marshal their resources. We've all asked for a few more minutes when staring at a menu. But all of these GMs and front office personnel are where they are to make difficult decisions. They have proprietary data and internal analysts dedicated to understanding their position relative to the rest of the league, and how any move in the here and now impacts their long-term vision. To complain (if that report is accurate) that over half the season is not enough to properly assess their season is bullshit of the highest order. Move the deadline, and you'd simply have increasingly discounted trade offers because teams would be acquiring even less control of anyone they're acquiring, rental or not.

Major league front offices are behaving like the managers they lampooned two decades ago. They're effectively sacrificing a runner to second in the ninth inning—not because it's the correct move, but rather because it is safe. It used to be that the phrase "moral hazard" was used to describe general managers who made ill-fated, short-sighted decisions aimed at locking in wins and securing their jobs at the expense of their team's future. Now, general managers are guilty of committing moral hazards in the opposite direction, playing it utterly safe and terrified of becoming scapegoats.

In lieu of bold action, they opt to pussyfoot around a current window of contention, choosing instead to play the long game and stack up years of control like they're blocks in a game of Jenga. GMs pass on signing quality players in free agency because the back-end of the deal might look bad, and because they might be able to squeeze out 70 percent of the production from a player who costs a tenth as much. That's a safer investment, too, because it's also hard to prove a negative—it's impossible to prove that Manny Machado would make the Mets a playoff team in 2019-2020, but it's easy to say that the back half of Robinson Cano's contract sucks. Owners, who rule over GM's jobs, are also humans with human brain processes that will always make the so-called albatross contract uglier than the road not taken.

These days, GMs are remembered for the bad deals they make and the surplus value they generate, not the acquisition of expensive, necessary talents that meet their market worth (or fall slightly short while still providing significant on-field value). And front offices know that one or two expensive misfires can cost them their jobs, no matter how many good deals they make.

No front office exemplifies this ethos more than the Toronto Blue Jays. General Manager Ross Atkins had this to say following the Blue Jays underwhelming trade deadline:

This is by no means the first time that an executive will cite years of control to justify their actions, which is often just another way of saying "don't look at what we got, look at how much we got of it." Atkins touts quantity to elide the discussion of quality—either, that of the players acquired, or those given up. Remember: the other teams presumably value years of control, too.

Atkins also had some thoughts to offer regarding free agents back in early 2018:

Miami Marlins 2020

This ignores, of course, whether the player can create enough value in the front end of a contract to justify the longer term of a deal, and the decline that often occurs in the back end. It also ignores whether the player can fill a need the team requires and put them in a position to compete for and win a championship. But as teams seemingly avoid contention at all, where they might end up having to consider and later justify some of these tough decisions, we still see risk-averse approaches.

Anthony Fenech's article on two trades that recently extended GM Al Avila didn't make got at this issue rather well:

> Passing on those deals was defensible: Both players had yet to break out and trading [Michael] Fulmer—a pitcher who appeared to be a future ace, no matter his injury concerns—would have taken serious gumption, opening Avila up to strong criticism.

Avoiding strong criticism is something each of us can understand as a motivation, but the avoidance of criticism only matters if that criticism is valid. In Fulmer's case, shoving his injury concerns aside affects not only the years that the team controls him (he is currently missing a full season due to Tommy John surgery) but also the quality of those seasons, as his knee and elbow injuries combined to dampen his effectiveness even when healthy enough to pitch. But it was easy to present the then-current image of Fulmer as a top of the rotation pitcher who the team had under its domain for the next five seasons as something to build around. The status quo isn't nearly as often second-guessed as a decision that disrupts it.

⚾ ⚾ ⚾

MLB GMs are risk-averse to a fault. They are ivy-educated and consulting firm-approved, and yet they can't seem to avoid leaving wins on the table in their all-consuming lust for a non-existent $/WAR championship. They are supposed to zig when everyone else zags, and not merely pay lip service to the idea of zigging through a calculated PR plan built on convincing the fan base their approach is novel when it actually apes most of their competitors. Instead they've become far more concerned with making safe, accepted-by-the-new-common-wisdom decisions, such that our prior understanding of what a moral hazard is has become inverted.

I can't blame them entirely, and not only because of the reasons that Quinton illuminated in his article, but also because of the damage wrought by the introduction of the second wild card (WC2) spot. MLB's desire to have more teams in playoff contention has sparked anti-competitive behavior. Teams know now that they do not need to swing big as they assemble their roster because there is a good chance that a mediocre team can either catch fire and capture a division, or muddle along until they back into the WC2.

Simultaneously, the one-game playoff has neutered the WC1, putting an entire season on the flip of a coin like some sort of baseball-obsessed Anton Chigurh. While the one-game playoff makes sense as a way to increase the value of winning a division, it also means that if a front office doesn't like its chances of overcoming a behemoth like the Dodgers or Astros in the offseason, they have few incentives to chase glory. Similarly, the relative inaction in the NL Central at the trade deadline—despite a wide open division—can be explained by the idea that any high-variance investment could still result in only a wild card (or worse) result, given the mere two months left in the season to make an impact.

⚾ ⚾ ⚾

As stated at the top, we should not confuse reasons for excuses. The implementation of the second wild card is just one of many environmental factors that influence how each front office operates. I am convinced that it is one of the larger factors, but I am also convinced that organizations need to shed the yoke of "efficiency at all costs" so that they can instead pursue competition, as the spirit of the game intends. Until they do, we're all deadline losers.

—*Craig Goldstein is an author of Baseball Prospectus.*

Index of Names

Aguilar, Jesús 20
Alcantara, Sandy 50
Alfaro, Jorge 22
Anderson, Brian 24
Banfield, Will 78, 107
Berti, Jon 26
Bleday, JJ 79, 96
Boxberger, Brad 52
Brigham, Jeff 54
Brinson, Lewis 28
Cabrera, Edward 86, 98
Castillo, Wilkin 91
Cervelli, Francisco 30
Chen, Wei-Yin 56
Chisholm, Jazz 80, 97
Conley, Adam 58
Cooper, Garrett 32
Dean, Austin 91
Devers, Jose 103
Díaz, Isan 36
Diaz, Lewin 91, 100
Dickerson, Corey 34
Dugger, Robert 60, 106
Edwards, Storm 106
Encarnacion, Jerar 104
Galloway, Isaac 91
Garcia, Yimi 93
Garrett, Braxton 87, 102
Granderson, Curtis 38
Guzman, Jorge 88, 100
Harrison, Monte 81, 99
Heineman, Tyler 91
Hernandez, Elieser 62
Holloway, Jordan 93, 105
Joyce, Matt 40
Kemp, Matt 91
Kintzler, Brandon 64
Kolek, Tyler 93
López, Pablo 66
Marrero, Deven 91
Mejia, Humberto 93
Mesa, Victor Victor 82, 102
Mesa Jr., Victor 91
Misner, Kameron 83, 101
Neidert, Nick 89, 103
Nunez, Nasim 91, 105
O'Brien, Peter 91
Prado, Martín 42
Puello, Cesar 91
Quijada, Jose 93
Ramirez, Harold 44
Riddle, JT 91
Rivera, Yadiel 91
Rogers, Trevor 93, 101
Rojas, Miguel 46
Sanchez, Jesus 85, 97
Sanchez, Sixto 90, 95
Scott, Connor 84, 104
Sharp, Sterling 93
Sierra, Magneuris 91
Smith, Caleb 68
Smith, Josh 93

Miami Marlins 2020

Solarte, Yangervis 91
Stanek, Ryne 70
Steckenrider, Drew 72
Stewart, Will 93
Ureña, José 74
Venditte, Pat 93
Vesia, Alex 93, 105
Villar, Jonathan 48
Wallach, Chad 91
Yamamoto, Jordan 76